CW01667527

SCHOOL DAYS AT CHATSWORTH

A PERSONAL MEMOIR OF THE WAR YEARS

by

NANCIE PARK

Remembering with gratitude
the welcome Penrhos College
received in 1939

This book is dedicated
to the memory of
the 10th Duke of Devonshire
1895–1950
and his wife Mary
1895–1988

I would like to pay special
tribute to our Headmistress at Chatsworth
Miss Constance Smith (1904–1992), who guided
us with dignity and love through
those dark years of war.

ACKNOWLEDGEMENTS

I would like to thank Her Grace the Duchess of Devonshire for her help and encouragement during the past year. Had it not been for her co-operation and enthusiam I would not have completed this book.

My thanks also go to Mr Ash Withers for his patience and help during my visits to The House.

And to many other people at Chatsworth not mentioned individually who have given their time and help, especially Mr Peter Day, Mr Michael Pearman and Mr Eric Oliver.

I am greatly indepted to Miss Betty Ley for so generously allowing me to reproduce part of her diary which she kept when a school girl at Chatsworth.

To Miss Monica Beardsworth and Mrs Joan (Fazakerley) Kerr who have both given me invaluable information, corrected many inaccurracies. I thank them both most sincerely for all their time and help.

And Miss Monica Beardsworth for allowing me to reproduce excepts from her book "Penrhos College the Second Fifty Years".

And Miss Constance Smith for allowing me to quote from her writings in the Penrhos Centenary Magazine.

To Lady Elizabeth Cavendish for allowing me to reproduce her article in the 1940 Penrhosian Magazine.

To Mrs Jean (Brett) Reddaway for allowing me to reproduce her sketch of the statues in the 1940 Penrhosian Magazine.

I would like to thank His Grace and the Chatsworth trust for allowing the E. I. Halliday painting on the cover of the book.

Macmillan London for allowing me to reproduce excepts from Her Grace's book "The House".

And also Mrs M. Shimwell, Mr B. Link, Mrs E. I. Oliver and Miss I. Solymossy who have all granted me interviews, and told me so much about the past.

I would like to thank Mr Michael Brailsford for his advice and help in the editing of this book.

And Mr Michael Coffey who has been so helpful in the publishing of this book.

My thanks also to Mr Jim Brown and Miss F. Bang for all their help and patience with my numerous corrections, much of the eventual publication I owe to them.

PHOTOGRAPHY

The majority of the photographs in this book, were taken by Mr Clement Hovey who died in 1954, and I am grateful both to the girls who have lent me their personal photographs and to Chatsworth for allowing me to use many of these from their archives.

The following have lent me their personal photographs: Penrhos College, Miss Monica Beardsworth, Mrs Margaret (Irwin) Watson, Mrs Cynthia (Rogers) Wilkinson, Mrs Anita (Kay) Hough, Mrs M. Shimwell, Mr B. Link. Thanks also to my husband Eddie, for all the recent photographs taken both inside The House and in the gardens.

© all rights reserved Nancie Park 2003

First published in 1986 by A. Quick & Co. under ISBN 0 9504912 2 5
Reprinted in 1994 and 1998 by Derbyshire Countryside Ltd.

Reprinted in 2003 by

DERBYSHIRE COUNTRYSIDE LIMITED

Heritage House, Lodge Lane, Derby, DE1 3HE. Tel: 01332 347087

ISBN 0 85100 117 3

CONTENTS

First term at Chatsworth September 1939, cars delivering girls and trunks outside the North entrance.

INTRODUCTION

Great Britain was never invaded during World War II, but Chatsworth House most certainly was.

Visitors, seeing The House today, restored to its former splendour would probably be surprised to learn that forty years ago in 1946, it was recovering from its war work.

The invasion consisted of two hundred and fifty boarding school girls, and thirty-six staff. The girls ranged in age from eleven to eighteen years, and they all lived in The House from 26th September 1939 to 21st March 1946, when, after the Easter Holidays, they returned to Colwyn Bay.

Penrhos College, a girls' boarding school, founded in 1880, is situated on the sea front in Colwyn Bay. Consisting then of about 320 girls, the 250 Senior and Middle School lived in two main buildings and 70 Juniors lived in a large house, 15 minutes walk away in Oak Drive.

Penrhos College before the war.

Penrhos College Colwyn Bay, science block and assembly hall.

In the Summer of 1939, the prospect of war with Germany was becoming more certain. To quote from Miss Monica Beardsworth's book "Penrhos College The Second 50 Years". *"The last meeting held at the end of the July term followed its customary pattern, but finally, and almost casually, (for in that end of term atmosphere one was disinclined to be alarmist), it was agreed that, should hostilities break out during the holiday period, all the staff would return at once to Penrhos".*

On 3rd September, with no room left for doubt, they one by one made their way back to Colwyn Bay.

What they did not know, however, was that the Ministry of Food had commandeered the main school for their own use. They had to have a comparatively safe place to work out the difficult problem of feeding wartime Britian. Only Professor Yorke — a Governor of the School, and Miss Smith, the Headmistress, and in only her 2nd year as Head, knew of this decision and they were ordered to keep this a secret until the plans were confirmed.

The staff swarmed back to school, imagining there was an immense amount to do. With every window, and every skylight, in each of the school buildings requiring a black-out, Westfield Dining Hall was hurriedly turned into a highly organised factory for cutting and hemming what appeared to be miles of black sateen.

As the term was due to start in around two weeks and before that the blackout must be complete, work naturally started early, and went on late. And yet to their astonishment Miss Smith repeatedly appeared and urged them to down tools and take time off. Trying to conceal their private belief that she had taken leave of her senses, they declined and went on measuring and machining until one morning they were summoned to attend an emergency staff meeting and the astounding news that they would soon be homeless was revealed."

The problem of re-housing Penrhos had been in the hands of Professor Yorke. As Professor of Tropical Medicine at Liverpool University and, as the foremost living authority on malaria, and sleeping sickness, the Government, prior to, and at the beginning of the war, was using his work increasingly to safeguard the health of the troops in the Tropics, and the demands this made on his time and energy were enormous.

The post card obtainable from "Book Room", we sent it whenever possible to parents and friends, proudly showing off our gracious war-time home.

Penrhos College assembly hall before the war.

After forty years many unknown facts of World War II are only just beginning to emerge. It is now known that Miss Smith heard about the possibility that the school would be commandeered as early as 1938. In a recent communication, Miss Smith can reveal "I remember distinctly getting a letter in the holidays marked "PRIVATE". Inside was a second envelope marked "MOST SECRET". Inside that was a letter from Sir Patrick Duff of the Office of Works (as then it was , not yet a Ministry) saying that if war came, our buildings would be taken over. I was not to tell *anyone;* if I wanted to tell my Chairman of Governors, I was to write back for permission. I remember that the letter came on Christmas Eve, 1938.

No one else could be taken into their confidence, and it was consequently very unobtrusively that Professor Yorke and Miss Smith set off on a series of excursions to discover if they could find a wartime home that might be possible, if Penrhos were dispossesed.

Meanwhile, far away in Derbyshire, another much larger building was preparing for change. Chatsworth House in Derbyshire, the home of the Duke and Duchess of Devonshire, was too spacious to remain a family home. In those wartime years, the Government decided that more use had to be made of the accommodation which Chatsworth provided.

In her book "The House", the present Duchess quotes, "The Duke made arrangments for Penrhos to take the House when he thought war was inevitable, realising that a girls' school would make far better tenants than soldiers". So Penrhos was offered the sanctuary of Chatsworth House, for the duration of the war. They gratefully accepted it, and the upheaval began.

Admiration for this mammoth task, must be felt for all the people concerned. From the Duke and Duchess who lent their precious heritage, to the organisers who managed to fit so many bodies into the House and live a fairly normal school life.

Although it must have been a daunting prospect, hundreds of beds, chairs, wardrobes, cookers, desks, dressing tables and other impedimenta had to be transported and fitted into Chatsworth, so that the staff and girls could exist in some kind of order. Miss Beardsworth writes:

"Initially there were a few problems, with the Ministry. They agreed to

The library in dust sheets during our occupation.

loan twenty or thirty lorries, which we could use to ferry all the paraphernalia to Chatsworth. These vehicles would travel day and night, between Colwyn Bay and Chatsworth, with a view to accomplishing the entire move within a matter of ten days.

There were other battles to be fought. The Ministry saw no need for wardrobes! and surely one chair per girl, and a solitary piano would be enough?

We eventually took twenty six pianos, and an adequate number of chairs, and wardrobes. But there remained the vexed question of rain damage to goods travelling in open lorries. The thought of soaked mattresses, and bedding, and of dripping stationery was too much to bear; there might be a war on, but even so, some degree of commonsense was essential! At last the Ministry agreed to provide a number of furniture vans, and the great pack up got under way with the minimum of delay.''

Before the school could move into Chatsworth there was a vast amount of work to be done in the House: clearing away beautiful furniture, carpets, and treasures.

To add to this task many immovable things had to be covered and protected. Chandeliers were enveloped in cloth, precious panelling was covered with boards, four poster beds draped with sheeting, and anything that could be moved stored away in either the Library, The Chapel, or the room next to the Orangery. (The Sculpture Gallery).

This amazing feat was accomplished by the Chatsworth staff in just eleven days. And to add to this there was also the dismantling of the remains of the 21st Birthday celebrations of the Marquess of Hartington — tragically killed in action later in the war in 1944.

Lord Hartington had actually come of age in December 1938 but, owing to the death of his Grandfather the 9th Duke, the festivities had been postponed until August, 1939.

So by the time the first staff from Penrhos set a tentative foot in the door of Chatsworth, things were definitely starting to move.

Meanwhile, Miss M. L. Edman the Deputy Headmistress, and Miss F. M. Dodd, the History and English mistress, were preparing for their first visit to Chatsworth. I quote from her own words published in the 1940 Penrhosian Magazine.

"On Sunday morning September 10th 1939, Miss F. M. Dodd and I drove from Bakewell to Chatsworth.

Near Sandy's Turn we wondered if we had by chance overlooked Chatsworth. We made enquiries of a native. With a broad grin he assured us that if we drove on a few yards we couldn't miss it.

A turn to the left, and there it was — square and massive, and far too imposing for us.

Panic-stricken, I switched off the engine, and gazed at that dignified pile. I felt it would never submit to becoming a homely school. It looked gracious in the autumn sunlight, but very detached. It had a secret life of its own, a tradition of which I knew nothing, and I was afraid of it.

But we must brave it somehow, so we drove slowly towards it.

The Lodge gates looked threatening. It seemed effrontery to drive through them. A glance at the façade that greeted us completed our discomfiture. We wilted through the front door.

A blur of red carpet, flowers, men converging upon us — then a nightmarish walk through the House.

One stately room after another, priceless pictures and carvings, handpainted wallpapers, rich canopied beds, dignified gilt chairs, quaint tapestries, a glimpse through windows of rolling parkland, formal lakes, statues and fountains — this could have no connection with Penrhos.

The names of the rooms too brought a feeling of incongruity — the Leicester Room. The Stag Parlour. The Red Velvet Room. The Yellow Drawing Room. The Leather Room.

Clutching at a straw of reality, I took out my copy of an old plan of Chatsworth. Surely if I followed it, and identified rooms with it, this formless grandeur would take shape and fall into some kind of order.

But it was a very old plan. Many additions had been made. The names had been changed since it had been printed. It merely added to my demoralization. The House refused to be subjugated.

Surely the owners should have been proud and haughty, unbending like itself, angry at this intrusion.

But they were welcoming and reassuring, most gracious and helpful, too human and sympathetic to be the real owners of the place. It was all most confusing.

A return to a hotel to a room with an exaggerated blackout, brought us back to reality.

I had borrowed the blue prints of the buildings. Late at night and early in the morning, in a depressing glimmer of light, I toiled at making sketch plans — and the House seemed bigger than ever.

It was a discouraging beginning for a black Monday. Then we were informed that the hotel was "Taken by the Military" and could no longer harbour us. So, homeless, and with a few sandwiches for lunch, we set off for Chatsworth once more.

There, we were greeted with a telegram laconically informing us "Mattresses arrive ten o' clock Tuesday morning."

We got to work in good earnest.

We systematically followed the sketch plans, and learnt a floor at a time. We must have been a dreadful nuisance to everybody. We burst into rooms inhabited by the family. We got in the way of the Chatsworth men, who were spiriting away their valuable furniture. We asked innumerable questions. Once we had mastered the building, we thought all would be easy. We could first write on the plan what each room would be used for. But it did not work out like that.

The wallpapers, the fire-places, the pictures, the books, had all to be considered. Staff only could be trusted to inhabit certain rooms, and prefects others.

There was also uncertainty about the numbers we must house. The Government was casting covetous eyes at the Junior School, and at a moments notice we might have to make room for seventy more people.

We paced up and down corridors, wondering if they could be turned into bedrooms and gazed at ornate bedrooms, wondering if they could be turned into classrooms.

Footsore and famished by night-time, we were most kindly offered a refuge in the Vicarage. We can not have been enlivening guests!

Tuesday was a stirring day. First, ten quarry-men arrived to carry furniture. Chatsworth looked at their hobnailed boots — and they were despatched.

Lorries swept up with horrible punctuality. The Orangery was soon piled high with mattresses, bedsteads, chests, and wardrobes.

Men tramped incessantly with loads of furniture down the long Bachelors' corridor.

But in spite of their labours, the Orangery grew fuller and fuller and overflowed into the garden.

We sped round the building trying to find nooks for twenty six pianos, for the reference library books, for innumerable desks: then to the laundry for the domestic science; to the stables to find a chemistry lab; and to the squash court for a gymnasium.

Day after day, the tide of furniture swept in, and the men tramped monotonously from seven in the morning to seven at night.

At one point we seemed lost in an avalanche of chairs — chairs from the Hall, chairs from the Reference Library, chairs from the sitting-rooms, the studies, the bedrooms, the dining halls. The only word we seemed to be hearing was "Where?"

I shall not easily forget my first night in Chatsworth.

The blackout was not then complete, so most of the building must be in darkness.

We crept along lonely dark corridors. Impassive statues loomed at us suddenly. We threaded our way round stranded wardrobes and derelict chairs and found ourselves in the place we had started from.

As I came from my room in the Cavendish wing, I switched on my torch to light up the long corridor. It was answered at the far end by another torch gleaming wickedly at me. Who could be there? It was only the reflection of my torch in the glass of a picture!

We slept on mattresses on the floor. At midnight, a sudden vibration, a pad, pad along the corridor, echoing through the stillness, the sound as of a key turning! What now? But it was only the faithful night watchman, doing his nocturnal round of the House.

In a fortnights' time on 26th September 1939 how different was the scene! The girls had returned to their new school. Each had their allotted place at Penrhos. School routine went on as usual in class-room, dormitory, dining-hall and common room.

After the first few days, we had settled. We worked as hard and as contentedly, as at Penrhos.

The House had accepted us, and accommodated us in Royal fashion".

The Duchess of Devonshire 1939.

Lady Elizabeth Cavendish and her cousin Catherine Macmillan eventually became boarding pupils at Penrhos for the first years of the war. Lady Anne Cavendish and Sarah Macmillan, (their younger sisters) lived at nearby Churchdale, and were tutored by their Governess Miss Bazeley.

However, Lady Anne and Sarah Macmillan came to the school for some games and to attend Guide meetings on Thursday afternoons. Lady Anne was in C Company, and as she was in my age group we did quite a few Guide activities together.

They all came to the house parties and film shows in the Painted Hall.

In 1940 Lady Elizabeth wrote this following piece for the school magazine.

Lady Elizabeth and Lady Anne Cavendish 1939.

CHATSWORTH IN WARTIME

by Elizabeth Cavendish

"When we knew that a school was going to Chatsworth, we all thought it was an awful nuisance, but now we have changed our minds.

Miss Smith, Dr Yorke, and Mr Hovey came over just before the war broke out to see if Penrhos could all get in. They decided it could, and then nothing happened until the Saturday before the war.

First, all the passage carpets were taken up, then the furniture and carpets in the rooms, and everything seemed in the most frightful muddle, except our bedrooms, Mummy's boudoir, and our school room where we had our meals.

On the day war was declared, we heard Mr Chamberlain's speech in the yellow drawing room, which had no furniture of any sort or kind in it, except the wireless which stood in the corner of the room.

We saw Miss Edman a few days after the war began, and when she had decided how all Penrhos could get in, the tremendous move started.

It was great fun seeing the school furniture coming in: the dozens of bookshelves, desks, beds, and the piles of books everywhere.

In about a fortnight, however, everything was nearly straight, and we were wondering what the mistresses and girls would be like.

A day or two afterwards we moved to Churchdale, and everything seemed very quiet.

The next time we saw Chatsworth there were several mistresses there, and the whole place looked better! Soon afterwards it was full of girls: the gold and yellow drawing room, the dining room and state rooms were full of beds and chests of drawers.

We went over several times both in the holidays and the term, then we were invited to go and play games on Tuesdays, and go to Guides on Thursdays.

The first Thursday was awful as we knew nobody, but they were all very kind to us. We went to each of the Companies in turn to see which we liked best. Then Anne went to C Company, and I went to A Company.

Almost every week we were asked to go to Penrhos parties. These were great fun, although it seemed funny to see so many chairs, and a film in the Painted Hall.

This term the gardens have had to be altered. There are tennis courts on the front lawns, and girls swimming in the ponds.

Chatsworth is much gayer than it used to be."

Cascade and steps in winter 1940.

FIRST DAY AT CHATSWORTH

26th September 1939 was a great day in the history of Penrhos College. It was the first day of the new term and also the first day of their residence in Chatsworth House. Girls arrived from all over the country, by coaches which had met trains, and by car if one had either enough petrol, or lived in the vicinity. The first view of the House brought gasps of amazement, for a few seconds they were speechless — but these few seconds were probably the last time that tongues were stilled during the seven years in residence. Suddenly everyone began to talk at once.

It was a glorious Autumn day and the Cascade, plus all the fountains, including the famous and very impressive Emperor on Canal pond, had been turned on in welcome. As they walked up the drive and in through the North Hall entrance a large fire blazed in the fireplace on their left. Miss Beardsworth in her book quotes *"There were so many questions to ask, so much to find out, to explore, but first where must they go? and where would they sleep? In groups they were led to their dormitories, in groups they were taken to tea, by supper time most of them had an idea of the layout of their new home."* Nevertheless it was extremely difficult to imagine how they would all eat, sleep, have lessons and

Emperor and Seahorse fountains.

generally live in this magnificent setting.

As well as the usual "three R" subjects there were the three sciences (Biology, Chemistry and Physics) Art, Languages, Dancing, P.E. (then referred to as "Gym"), plus all the extra subjects of Elocution and Music, etc; we were a very musical school — hence the twenty six pianos. But it was wartime and we were lucky to be so safely ensconced in this enviable place so we fitted in and everyone found a niche in some corner of The House and managed to live a very normal school life. I was a small and extremely unsophisticated child of eleven years, who arrived at this strange place and school and was quite unprepared for such a shattering experience. But I can now look back over the years with many happy memories and am indeed very grateful to have had the privilege of living in Chatsworth House. The Duke and Duchess were very trusting in allowing us to use almost every part of the House and the complete freedom of the Gardens, Woods, and Park. Only the famous and valuable library was closed, but even in a corner of the ante-library, girls had private piano lessons.

The Devonshires private chapel, a most beautiful room, was also used for piano lessons but we didn't use it as a chapel. Much of the Devonshire's furniture was stored here, so there was not much space to spare. Many of the treasures were stored, but many were left, and we were soon passing priceless paintings and other valuable works of art without a second thought. In fact I think we all became rather blasé and never realised how lucky we were. Our parents and friends who visited, when petrol allowed, were much more impressed.

Of course a few rules were imposed to try to ensure the minimum damage to the House. Dustless chalk was used on the blackboards and sand was sprinkled on the floors before sweeping. All school work was done in pencil. Only the VIth form were allowed to use ink in a fountain pen — no inkwells. Also running indoors was a real and punishable sin.

Chatsworth House is so vast that I think it took me at least a month to become familiar with all its different rooms and corridors, not to mention the 13 bathrooms. More bathrooms were made after we left.

I quote from the Duchess of Devonshire's book "The House", published in 1982.

"The roof is 1.3 acres. There are 175 rooms, of which 51 are very big

indeed, 96 of more or less normal size, 21 kitchens and workshops and 7 offices connected by 3,426 ft of passage. 17 stair-cases and 359 doors — all lit by 2,084 electric light bulbs. There are 397 external window frames, 62 internal window frames, 5 roof lanterns and 60 roof lights with a grand total of 7,873 panes of glass. 24 baths, 52 wash-hand basins, 29 sinks, 53 lavatories, and 6 wash-ups complete the unusual statistics. The total cubic living space in Chatsworth is 1,704,233 cubic feet. The total cubic living space in a first-time buyers modern two bedroomed house is 4,726 cubic feet. So you could fit 365 such houses into Chatsworth. The Painted Hall could contain 10.45. The Great Dining-room 8.3 and the Sculpture Gallery 14.23 houses."

Deer in Chatsworth Park.

Although we were allowed to go almost anywhere in the House and grounds Edensor and Baslow were out of bounds unless accompanied by parents or relatives.

Edensor only boasted one small shop but we never went inside Edensor village unless it was to attend Church.

Baslow had one or two small shops and hotels, at which some parents stayed when visiting. It was also convenient if a parent had no transport or was limited for time. A visit to Baslow was definitely a treat.

But a much bigger thrill was to visit Bakewell, or occasionally (before petrol rationing disallowed) Buxton.

Fairly soon after the the move to Chatsworth, Buxton became nearly as inaccessible as London — but Bakewell was possible.

An outing with parents to Bakewell was quite an event to be looked forward to with eager anticipation.

A few lucky girls receiving visitors before petrol became unobtainable.

To us it constituted "civilization". There were shops — plural, and the feeling of being let out into the world was very strong.

One of the main objects during these precious few hours was to have a meal — as good a meal as it was possible to have. Either lunch or high-tea, never an evening meal as we never stayed out late. Having satisfied our hunger, the next thing to be done was to comb the shops for anything edible which we could bear back to school in triumph, Cadburys drinking chocolate being a great prize. And as we shopped, we were perpetually looking out (as was anyone in Britain at that time) for such rare items as knicker elastic, pipe cleaners, which we used for hair curlers, small bottles of shampoo, or ever scarce stationery items, which the school shop did not stock.

A purchase of one or two of these things, and we returned to school refreshed and ready to do a few more weeks in isolation.

On reflection, I think, we were all rather obsessed by food, or sometimes the lack of it — I quote with Betty Ley's permission a piece from her diary written much later in the war when finding anything extra was considered a real prize. And as she was by then a member

The author's first form room.

of the VIth form she had extra facilities, fewer regulations, and so could 'forage'.

"I am writing this now by Stag Fire and it is Tuesday October 24th 1944, after half term and feeling a bit flat in a way. Yesterday we had a grand time. We could go out in the morning and afternoon, but had to be in for lunch.

In the morning I didn't bother to go out, just sat by Stag fire with a few others with the wireless on. But the rest of the crowd went to Baslow and bought grub and pop. We had school lunch and then came to Stag and fried sausages on the fire, amidst loud laughter, and then in the fat fried some tomatoes, and then some bread and fish paste and then our pop!! There was Mickey, Bucket, A.O. Jumbo, Pat, Liza and me. We were so hilarious that we were quite drunk, and someone made the pun "a doe party in Stag".

Well after we had finished gorging, we got ready and went across the park to Baslow for tea at 4.30!, which consisted of boiled eggs and bread and jam, scones, cakes, biscuits and tea.

Well we decided we couldn't walk back, so I went and ordered a taxi! and be damned if we didn't sail up to school in state! Laugh!!! it cost us 7/-! And then on the stroke of quarter to six when there was roll call and then supper — which was bacon on fried bread! And then a film and then bed!"

We were encouraged to bring bicycles from home and kept them stored in bicycle racks in the stables, occasionally having the bicycle saddles nibbled by the deer who used to stray into the stables looking for food! As bike riding was a completely new innovation for Penrhos, girls had to take a test to be sure they were capable of riding without damaging themselves. This test entailed a ride from the top of the stable hill to the bottom, with a sudden stop, to test the reliability of the brakes. Once having satisfied authority of our bicycling ability, we could ride anywhere in the Park. The choice of rides was limited and many times we found ourselves sitting at the boundary of the Park with a longing look at the main road. Nevertheless, it was an enjoyable and vigorous pastime in which we could indulge any afternoon, if not playing games.

As the war progressed, however, we mostly took bicycles home and left them there. Bikes were also extremely necessary to use in the holidays as our only means of transport. They became difficult to transport to

Setting off from the stables for a bicycle ride in the park.

A group of girls in the park.

and from school, so we opted to use them at home rather than at school.

When roaming around the park or woods we had to be in groups of not less than four girls. This was in case of an accident occuring. One girl would stay with the injured party and there still remained two girls who could go together for help. Also I suppose, there was an uncomfortable feeling felt by those in authority that there was a possibility of German parachutists descending from the skies. I'm sure that this was, at the time, a real and frightening thought, but I clearly remember giggling about such a castastrophe after "lights out" with a sort of horrified thrill. I have a sneaking suspicion that a few girls might have found it to be a diversion in our all female world.

Much later we learned that the Dowager Duchess had taken our Headmistress to a remote valley in the hills, with large caves, in which she thought she might hide the whole school if invasion came. "The caves", Miss Smith said, "thank heaven were not needed, but in an Antwerp garage after the war, invasion maps were found, going either side of Chatsworth." At that time invasion was not just a possibility — but it was expected that it would probably happen.

I vividly remember a visit to Strutt's Cafe — now Ivy House — in Baslow. We adored going to Strutt's, where we could buy ham and eggs, (really thick ham) and it was a most delicious high tea. It was a great treat, and the first time I went, I was very struck by a text on the wall. It was an old text which was obviously been there a few years, and it said "DONT WORRY IT MAY NEVER HAPPEN". I remember thinking of being invaded by the Germans, and thinking to myself IF only that text were true — but I know it *will* happen. So *that* awful threat hung over us all, and I suppose as it was such a terrible one, all our discomforts or inconveniences became very unimportant as the whole country concentrated on keeping alive and the German army from invading our shores.

Meanwhile the Duke and Duchess of Devonshire and their family moved to live at Churchdale for the duration of the war — a smaller Devonshire home a few miles away. The Dowager Duchess lived in Edensor, at Edensor House. She was a frequent visitor to the House — a gracious figure, who never spared herself showing servicemen round the house, particularly the Americans who were billeted in the area. In 1947 she moved back to Hardwick so that the present Duke and Duchess and their family could move into Edensor House. They lived in Edensor House until 1959 when they took up residence at Chatsworth. So for twenty long years the House was uninhabited by the Devonshire family. I'm sure it welcomed them home joyfully.

The West Hall — 'Foot Class' was held here.

We were extremely conscious of our good fortune in living at Chatsworth; and gradually came to know The Duchess, and Dowager Duchess as they visited the House. The Duchess will always be remembered for her kindness and good humour. We loved to see her, and many of the staff and girls with whom she came into contact, remember her with great affection.

The Dowager Duchess was equally charming, but I think we were rather in awe of her. An upright Victorian figure, she would walk across the Park from Edensor House, carrying an umbrella, and often accompanied by a little dog. I quote from Betty Ley's diary. *"2nd February. Went for a nice walk with Bucket, along the road to Edensor. We met the Dowager and her 'peke', and stopped and had quite a long conversation. She was pointing up to the Hunting Tower and Duke's Seat with her brolly, and nearly poked Bucket's eye out! How we laughed afterwards. We felt it wasn't everybody that went out for a walk and hobnobbed with Dowagers!"*

Frozen Cascade 1940.

Frozen pond in garden 1940.

Another event concerning the Devonshire family was when the late Marquess of Hartington contested a seat in Parliament against a local Alderman, Charlie White. No one waited more eagerly for the result than the girls of Penrhos. I remember sitting with several other girls, on bicycles at the Beeley gates, beseeching any passer-by to tell us "news of the election". Naturally, we were all, without exception, bitterly disappointed when Lord Hartington failed to win the seat.

The present Duke and Duchess — when they were Lord and Lady Andrew visited Chatsworth after their marriage. They were accompanied by the Duchess of Kent, and Mr Hovey was ready with his camera to record the event with a charming photograph.

The present Duke and Duchess of Devonshire after their marriage, as Lord and Lady Andrew visiting Chatsworth with the Duchess of Kent.

THE PAINTED HALL

The magnificent Painted Hall was the centre and heart of the school. Here, morning and evening chapel was held and it was also the assembly hall. The choir sat on the stairs and the rest of the school in rows on chairs in the body of the hall. An organ at the bottom of the stairs near the fireplace and a raised platform and lectern in front of the curtain at the entrance made this the best of all the improvised rooms. I'm sure that it was even better than any purpose built assembly hall. It had atmosphere and we loved it. The fascinating painted ceiling was a constant source of interest, especially if concentration waned during the sermon in chapel.

Morning chapel always consisted of a hymn, lesson, psalm, prayers and blessing. At the end of this short service, we waited, hoping that our Headmistress would say "please will you sit". This meant that she had one, or even more tit-bits of information to impart — (rather like having the postman). If she swept out of the hall without a word we all felt some small sense of disappointment, but usually there was a small item of news to impart and we were duly satisfied.

It was a most formal occasion. After the staff and girls had assembled we waited in awed silence for Miss Smith. She would walk down the oak stairs preceded by her head girl who carried her prayer book and "arrive" on the platform beside the lectern.

The service only lasted about twenty minutes but it was a vital part of school life and the beautiful Painted Hall gave the ceremony an added dignity. A modified version also took place every evening directly after supper.

One of the loveliest memories in my entire life, was to sit in the body of the hall at the Christmas carol service and listen to the choir. They would start singing the carol, "O little town of Bethlehem" two floors above in Picture Gallery and gradually the sound would come nearer as they wound down two flights of stairs to take their place on the steps. Nearer to Heaven no one could have felt at that carol service. Later, as a Senior, I joined the choir and could take part in this glorious occasion.

The hall was used on Saturday morning for "School Singing" which consisted of a rehearsal of next week's hymns and psalms or for any concert we might be performing such as the "Messiah" at Christmas and Easter.

The forbidden corridor and the window ledge, used as a hiding place on Hallowe'en.

After "School Singing" a history mistress took a subject called "Current Events" known to the school as "currants". This was to give the girls a resumé of news of the previous week. Obviously the news was mainly concerned with the war and with the help of a blackboard, coloured chalks and well-drawn maps, we followed the progress or retreat of the various armies.

The balcony running across the Painted Hall was out of bounds to all except mistresses, prefects, or the odd girl suffering with a sprained ankle. Possibly it was thought that a constant stream of two hundred and fifty bodies might make it unsafe. The only time I ventured onto this forbidden territory was for a dare on Hallowe'en night. The whole House was a marvellous place where a few brave spirits could don a sheet, and "ghost" round the corridors. For some reason the staff seemed to develop a form of deafness on that one night. We were hardly ever caught.

Probably the most popular use of the hall was as a picture house. On house party and occasionally other Saturday nights, a projector appeared; and we would sit enthralled, by a fairly old film. Stopping three or four times during the performance, to change the reel.

Painted Hall as assembly hall. Note the hassocks piled at the side, which the choir used for sitting on the steps.

Each of the four houses had a "House Party" where that particular house would "Entertain" the rest of the school. There were two house parties in each of the two winter terms. On these nights, the film would be followed by a special supper, with jelly and blancmange (a great treat). Then we would all repair to the theatre for a 'dance'. How we enjoyed those dances in our all female world! Whichever house was to be host, had been earnestly practising a group of its most musical girls for weeks before, to make a band. These girls were drilled into unison (or sometimes harmony), humming behind a comb, on to which toilet paper had been stretched. This, plus the best jazz piano player in the house, and perhaps a drum and a few percussion instruments, made an exceedingly proficient and effective noise.

This feast of delight was only surpassed by the Christmas party; the biggest event in the school calendar — entertainment-wise anyway. Consternation ranged on the first Christmas term at Chatsworth. Where could we hold "the dance?" The Theatre was not considered to be large enough for comfort. It was fine for a house party, but the dance was different. The Duke and Duchess came to the rescue. "Why not hold it in the dining room?" It had a proper ballroom floor, and they would order the protective coverings to be removed from the fireplace

The large dining room. A dormitory holding twenty five beds, and also the venue for the annual Christmas party.

and the great chandelier. This was soon accomplished, and the plans could go ahead. Very early after breakfast on the morning of the party the twenty five beds, mats, chairs, dressing tables, wardrobes etc, were trundled either into the corridor or anywhere out of sight. The dining room was decorated and festooned with all things colourful, plus holly and the usual greenery. The Duke and Duchess promised to attend, and the staff also came. Some or probably most of the staff even danced. We really were the centre of the world! No one attending this lovely party could ever forget the excitement of such an event in the humdrum life of school. The fact that we "dressed" — even the youngest girl at the beginning of the war had to have a party (and preferably long) dress as a compulsory part of the uniform, meant that we all felt very grand indeed. This Christmas party in the large dining room became an annual event throughout out stay at Chatsworth.

THE DORMITORIES

The sleeping arrangements were certainly different to that of a normal school. To me they were horrific, but some girls actually found them to be rather fun.

All three state rooms on both floors were used as dormitories, each holding many beds and other bedroom equipment. The Drawing room held 21 beds. The Music room 15 beds and the State bedroom 16 beds. As well as these large rooms, there was an even larger one which was the enormous dining room (of party fame) housing 25 girls. Other dormitories, which were smaller, only had eight beds and were much more popular. We changed "dorms" each term and I well remember the eager anxiety with which we scanned the lists on the notice board. It was the very first thing we did when we walked through the door at the beginning of term. Would we sleep in "Duchess" or "Den" or "Red Velvet"? three small very popular rooms on the first floor, and allocated to the juniors. Or would it be "Scots" or "Sabine"? to name but two on the second floor and given to the seniors.

My first term was spent in South Gallery, a corridor on the first floor, down which sixteen beds were spaced along its entire length.

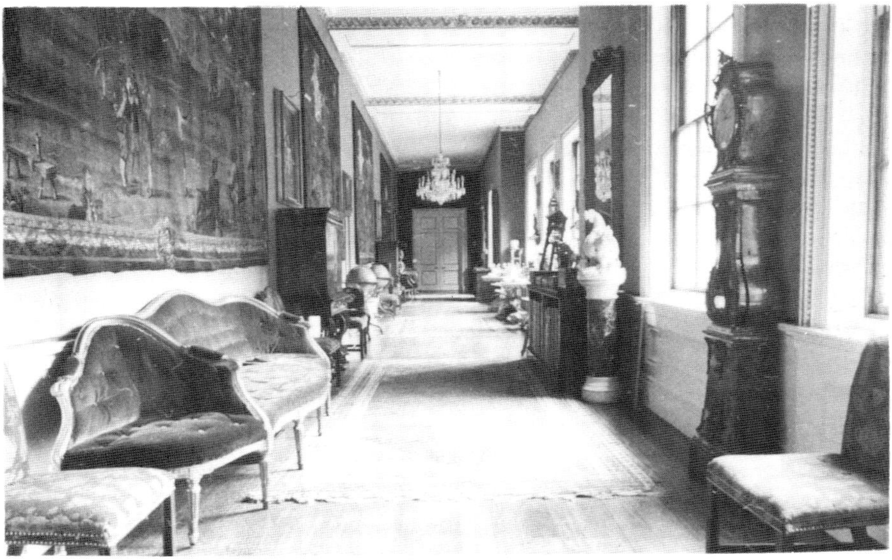

South Gallery, a corridor holding 16 beds, and the author's first dormitory.

Needing the bathroom in the middle of my first night, the journey entailed a long walk, out of the dormitory, down the Painted Hall stairs, past Stag Parlour, and into Chapel corridor to the toilets opposite the fireplace. These were the lavatories, and wash basins to which our ''Dorm'' had been allocated — No poaching on anyone else's loos, even if they were nearer. As I groped my way through the night with a flickering torch, a statue loomed into sight, and I was very relieved indeed to regain the safety of my bed — and to worry more than a little about the nights to follow.

During our stay there were thirteen bathrooms in Chatsworth and we used most of them in turn. There was a rota for each girl to have two baths per week. Each dormitory kept to its allocated bathroom for washing, but we were scheduled to bath anywhere in the House and had to stick firmly to that rota. ''Bachelors'', a bath of enormous proportions on Bachelors corridor, was one of the most popular venues. Five or six girls could, and often did (unofficially of course) bath together. We all lost any sense of shyness very early in our school career. ''Den'' was a bathroom with mirrors round the entire wall and ''Sunken'' was beneath floor level.

In these super-soap and shower days, two baths per week might sound rather unhygienic, but fuel was rationed and hot water was a precious commodity. Anyway, every morning, without fail, we strip-washed. Pyjama tops were dropped to the waist, even in the coldest weather, and flannel and soap applied with chattering teeth. There was no escape. A prefect or mistress stood at the door with an eagle eye. Nor was there any ducking out of the scheduled two baths. The rota was regularly checked and luke-warm water was not considered an adequate excuse for missing a bath.

Throughout Britain, people were asked to save fuel by only filling their baths with 5 inches of water. Some patriotic souls even painted a line round the bath to make sure they did not cheat. No such drastic measures for the baths at Chatsworth, but we all felt it our duty to try to keep to that measly 5 inches, and to this day I never relax in a deep bath without a slight feeling of guilt.

Hair washing took place on any and every week day night and the drying of hair was done round the three log fires: two in Chapel corridor and one in North entrance hall. Juniors started before supper at about 6p.m.; but the process went on until 10p.m. There was always *someone* drying their hair. Mobile hairdryers being a thing of the future for school girls, hair that had been left to dry by itself, around the fire, sometimes had to be seen to be believed! One could always spot the person at supper, who with red face and fly-away locks, had just come from a session round the log fire.

Trying to keep warm, at least in the two winter terms, posed many problems. There was some central heating, and sitting on the warm radiators (officially forbidden) or even clustering around them was some slight comfort. There was a fire in every form room, and the three "hair drying" fires, but with the intense cold of that first winter we were more often cold than warm, and chilblains flourished.

Betty Ley quotes from her diary. *"This last week we've had 24, 26, 28, + 30 degrees of frost and golly is it cold? There's tobogganning and skating. The laundry corridor was actually freezing this morning, as someone spilt water and it froze — Gee Whiskers!"*

We often slept in dressing gowns or siren suits, and occasionally put on a balaclava helmet, possibly as previous tenants of Chatsworth might have worn a tassled night cap. And every girl filled a rubber hot water bottle before she went to bed. I remember standing in line, as Nellie Jones, the Headmistresses maid and a very dear lady, stood beside a large geyser in the room near lower dining hall, and patiently filled them for us. Our "Hotties" as we referred to them were most precious, a leaking one being a major disaster, as with dressing gowns and bed socks, rugs and eiderdowns from home, we combated the cold. And if during the night the narrow school beds forced "Hottie" to obey the laws of gravity, it was probably found in the morning on the floor, a solid frozen lump.

These hotties also had another rather peculiar use. After lights out and before the hotwater bottles had succumbed to the cold, we would use them to revive failing torch batteries. We firmly believed that holding the batteries on the bottle for about ten minutes, resuscitated the batteries, giving them a few more precious minutes of life. Batteries and torch bulbs were scarce, but a very necessary part of existence in the black-out. Reading in bed, under the bedclothes, after lights out by torch-light, was a forbidden and great pleasure indulged in by most girls.

Bed making and unmaking was a strict 'ritual'. The beds, narrow, as were all school beds, had very thin, hard mattresses. There was a mania for "airing" these uncomfortable slabs and their bedclothes, seven days a week. It could be argued that with the general chill and draughts, everything was automatically "aired". However, authority decreed that each morning before breakfast, beds must be completely stripped. After depositing sheets, pillows, and blankets at the foot of the bed, a lunge was made at the mattress and it was made into the shape of a tunnel. The dormitories were inspected thoroughly during breakfast. A sudden "rapping" on the breakfast table and some poor absent minded named girl who had forgotten to dismantle her bed, was told to go and "hump the mattress" and in the process gathered bad marks against her house.

Chapel corridor. It had two log fires round which were grouped old sofas and chairs. A cosy place to sit, and also for drying hair.

Remaking the beds after breakfast was nearly as ritualistic. "Hospital corners" at the foot of the bed were smiled upon, and, in fact, obtaining one of the badges in the Girl Guides partly depended on the ability to do this. But all beds had to be completely tidy before morning school started and the bed-spreads turned up along each side of the bed, to assist the maids with the sweeping of the floors.

Dressing table drawers were frequently inspected, always without warning and good or bads marks given accordingly.

Twice, during each night the night-watchman made his slow, quiet and careful check round the house. He turned a key at various points along the route, which registered on a machine at the lodge, to say that all was well. They crept through each dormitory with little or no disturbance to the sleeping girls, although some insomniacs who were prepared for any diversion, often tried to engage these gentlemen in conversation. But they would refuse to be drawn and politely pretended that the girls weren't there. It would be interesting to hear some of their reminiscences now, but sadly, none are alive today.

All girls under 13 years had to rest on their beds after lunch (and before departing for the games field) for half an hour. Most girls read, wrote letters or occasionally fell asleep, but it was a good idea after our early 6.45 start to the day — with that terrible shattering, rising bell.

Machine at the lodge where the night watchman 'clocked in' from various points in the House during each night.

The beer cellar in 1939. It made an extremely good air raid shelter. We sat closely together in rows on forms and ate bovril and cream crackers during the bombing of Sheffield.

The beer cellar today.

Our health and safety was the first consideration both to our parents, and the school authority. It was in fact not the school's scholastic record, (good though it was), but a view of the beer cellars, which confirmed my Mother's mind in deciding to send my Sister and myself to Chatsworth. Both in an air raid or even invasion, she felt we would be safe. They were used several times during the early part of the war, when Sheffield had its pounding from the enemy. The whole school assembled in the cellars, packed tightly together on forms. Eventually cream crackers and Bovril would be passed down the rows until the all-clear was given and then we would return to our icy beds.

We also collected in the cellars on another occasion. It was on the evening that two German planes dived out of the sky, to machine gun The House. It was a beautiful evening in summer term 1942. Almost the entire school was gathered in the Painted Hall, where they had gone immediately after supper for evening prayers. Both dining halls — each holding two school houses, would walk in single file into the hall, as soon as supper was over. Sometimes there would be a slight gap in the assembling of the houses, as the two dining halls did not always finish at the same moment. This evening the gap between "Upper" and "Lower" dining hall arriving in the Painted Hall was quite considerable. The reason for this was that one unfortunate girl had managed to anoint herself with most of the contents of a bottle of milk. The girl was dispatched to Duchess bathroom on the North side, to repair the damage, and change her clothes, and by the time the table, form, and general area had been dried, at least five minutes had elapsed, as they hurried into evening prayers.

Miss Edman the Deputy Headmistress — who was known to be quite slow in her conducting of prayers, was coming to the end of the service, and a few keen tennis players were impatient to be out on the courts on the South Lawn. As she was actually saying "The peace of God, which passeth all understanding" *our* peace was shattered with a horrifying crashing noise.

In the first few seconds, the noise sounded exactly as if someone was falling down stairs, dropping a huge load of crockery. But in an instant it grew into a terrifying sound and we all thought our last moments had come. However, our emergency drill was good, and we all automatically headed for the beer cellar. We waited, trembling, for something else to happen but nothing did, and eventually word came through that the planes had been shot down in Lincolnshire. Naturally we all cheered, just as if we had won a hockey match!

The only other girls who were not in the Hall at the time were seven of the youngest girls in the school. Too young to be allowed in go into evening prayers, they all lived together in Den bedroom on the North side and went to bed immediately after supper. They were preparing for bed when they heard the planes, then actually saw the pilot. Realising what was happening, they dived for the floor underneath their beds.

A Matron and her friend were taking a walk in the park, when they had their view of the proceedings, from the ground, naturally, when they realised what was happening. Much later it emerged that there had been two German bombers, which had been attempting to bomb the D.P. battery works, in Bakewell. These works made the batteries for our submarines, so from a German point of view, it made good sense to put them out of action.

The planes should have taken their bearing on the river Wye, but instead of finding the Wye, they found the river Derwent, and headed

Machine gun bullet scars on the North wall.

for Chatsworth in error. Presumably even a faulty navigator had enough sense to realise that Chatsworth House couldn't by any stretch of the imagination be a battery factory. No doubt we should be grateful that the pilot of the planes disliked wasting bombs because they could easily have emptied their load onto The House during that summer evening.

As it turned out, they vented their disappointment by peppering the North side of the House with a few machine gun bullets, and the poor unfortunate girl drying her clothes in a bathroom on the North side, watched the attack with horror. Such is chance, and many girls were probably saved from an early death purely by one girl spilling milk on her dress, and so holding up prayers — because had prayers finished two minutes earlier, dozens of girls would have been outside enjoying free time, strolling in the garden or playing tennis before bedtime. As we were in the habit of filing straight out from prayers into the garden, many of us would have been a direct target for the planes.

The scars of those bullets on the North side of the House are still there today. Mrs Shimwell remembers Mr Shimwell (the Duke's Comptroller during our stay at Chatsworth) telling her, that after the planes had passed over, he picked up some of the girls black, woollen swimming costumes which had been left out to dry and they were riddled with holes! As a result of this safe deliverance from the attack, two parents launched a "Penrhos Special Appeal" to which other parents responded generously, and raised a large sum of money for the R.A.F. Benevolent Fund as a thanksgiving for their daughters' safety.

We had two other war incidents at Chatsworth.

One day a Wellington Bomber crashed in the Park on Lindup (between the Beeley traffic lights and Edensor). Mr Eric Oliver the Duke's present Comptroller remembers it happening. He was a small boy at the time, and was soon at the scene with a friend inspecting the wreckage and collecting bits of perspex as souvenirs.

The other event connected with the war, was the machine gunning of the East side of the House — an unfortunate error. American soldiers were having target practice on the moor behind the House. Suddenly bullets were spattering into the House on the East side, and further investigation showed the Chatsworth staff that the House had been omitted from the map which their allies possessed. They were not amused. This omission was very soon rectified, but not before a stray

The Hunting Tower — a roll call was taken here on days when the weather was unfit for games.

Orangery steps where we waited to be admitted after our wet walk.

bullet had lodged inside a table in the library where it remains to this day.

Living as we did in such close proximity, we seemed to attract germs and infections from anywhere and everywhere. Great care was taken to try to spot an early onset of an epidemic, and a sensible living regime was the order of the day. Exercise and fresh air, played a large part in the school curriculum. We all had to be out of doors every afternoon from 2p.m. to 4p.m. — wet or fine. Rare exceptions being either a broken or sprained limb, or a high temperature.

The uniform insisted on one set of water-proof clothing, including a rather fetching "mac-hat". It was made of stitched navy gaberdine and was a most pliable piece of headgear on which we could plant a tuck in the back and mould it to our individual shape. Authority, not feeling a mac-hat worthy of their disapproval, didn't seem to object. So equipped, they felt we could be exposed to the elements and suffer no harm.

Games were cancelled when it rained and instead we had to walk to the Hunting Tower at the top of the woods. Here, prefects took a roll call, and there was no clocking in by friends. Having achieved this marathon climb, we still had to wait outside, until the magic hour of 4p.m. Every girl must have memories of waiting on the steps of the Orangery for the doors to be opened to re-admit their wet and drooping figures.

Both Senior and Junior girls had their own "medicine room". This was a small room manned each morning and evening by a Matron after breakfast and supper. Here, we could go and "report sick", and have our temperatures taken, perhaps a boil 'lanced' or an ankle bandaged. Here, we also bought any chemist items and entered them in a book. At the end of term parents would receive a bill for our purchases. Some people felt genuinely ill; many just wanted an excuse for a lazy day, or to be 'excused' certain lessons. But the Matrons knew all the dodges, and malingering generally didn't work.

Those of us who were small and thin (as I was) were encouraged to take Radio Malt. We really did not need any encouraging; it was quite delicious, resembling treacle toffee. Each girl had her own named jar, and queued to receive one spoonful each night after supper. Rather as one now enjoys an after eight mint. Never has "one spoonful" been so widely interpreted. Whether it really helped our growth (I'm still small) or reduced infection is doubtful, but we were not going to argue the point, and ate it with relish.

For the first three weeks of every new term, Matron would creep into the form room during prep at about 6p.m. before supper. Armed with a bowl of pink fluid in which about six thermometers reposed, she would proceed down the row, sticking a thermometer into each girl's mouth. After a short time, the thermometers would be removed, and shaken with a fascinating flick of the wrist, put back into the pink fluid to frighten the germs, and recycled into more waiting mouths.

We were all, of course, supposedly immersed in 'prep' but never failed to notice the odd girl whose temperature registered concern on Matron's face. "Come to see me after supper, and I will take it again", had everyones' attention. Pneumonia, or an attack of 'flu had soon been allocated to the lucky victim. At least I always thought them to be lucky because the recipient of a second and persistent temperature was usually removed to the Sanatorium, or "San". This was the sick quarters situated in the Cavendish wing. It consisted of three marvellous small, quiet rooms, and a bathroom opposite the main drive. They are now used as offices for the Comptrollers and the secretaries. Here we were put to bed in rooms of only three or four girls, almost like home. Each room had an old fashioned fireplace with bars. Fires were lit before we were properly awake and at tea-time — absolute bliss. Those who were allowed out of bed could squat in front of the fire and make toast for all.

If we were lucky enough to be still in-situ at the weekend we could wave to friends below the windows who were congregating on the drive. They would be forming up in pairs to make a long crocodile which would wind its way to Edensor Church for Matins, so we looked down and gloated, and felt extremely smug. When the waiting girls were all present underneath the "San" windows, prefects passed down the line, handing each girl a silver three penny piece. (This was supposed to teach us that we must always give silver and never copper in a Church collection) This (now) antique coin, we duly deposited on the collection plate. After the sidesman had counted the coins, and received a cheque from the school, the three penny pieces were returned for redistribution the following week.

We went to Edensor Church nearly every Sunday morning for Matins, and those girls who had been confirmed, were encouraged to go to early communion service whenever they desired. It took, however, a great deal of will power to desert a warm bed on the one morning of the week on which we were allowed to stay in bed until 8a.m. as opposed to 6.45a.m.

Leaving Chatsworth for Matins winter 1940.

Returning to school for cold beef and beetroot.

on weekdays. Penrhos was a Methodist Foundation, and when the school was founded in 1880, most of the original pupils were of that creed. In 1940, however, about half the girls were Church of England, and the rest Methodist. So morning service was 'Church' almost always at Edensor, and the evening service was 'Chapel' and was held in the Painted Hall. In the evening we usually had a visiting Methodist preacher — sometimes from nearby Cliff College and many were amusing and interesting. We also parted with another three penny piece for the evening collection.

Sixpence for two church collections seems possibly rather mean but in those days one (old) penny bought a respectable bar of chocolate which would now cost about 11 new pence so we probably gave about 70p each week. Our weekly pocket money allowance was 1/8d. We didn't feel too deprived, there wasn't very much to spend it on. Stamps usually came from home and most stationery was put on the bill and chemist requirements were "signed for" in the special book.

There was a large cupboard at the bottom of the North Hall steps called "book room" although it wasn't a room. Here we could buy pencils, rubbers, note paper (headed with the Chatsworth address if we felt rich) and other small day to day items.

Mr Bert Link in the grapehouse.

But the things I felt were really worth saving for were the peaches and grapes in summer term. And if a visiting parent felt generous, we never refused the gift of a few extra pennies. Mr Link was in charge of all these delicious fruits in the Chatsworth greenhouses, a peach cost two shillings and about the same price for a bunch of grapes. They were worth *every* penny. One must remember that during the war, an orange was nearly unobtainable — very few ever arrived in Britain, so a single orange was probably enjoyed about twice a year (if we were lucky) And adults didn't stand a chance as the shops saved them for children. Bananas and lemons disappeared completely for the duration of the war. Fruit, such as we knew it, consisted of apples, pears, and plums from English orchards. And good as these were, they were not oranges, lemons, or bananas. So these home grown Chatsworth peaches and grapes were the caviare of fruit and only at Chatsworth were they easy to obtain.

In the fresh Derbyshire air, food was never far away from our minds. We had a healthy appetite and were lucky in having an extremely competent and resourceful domestic Bursar. She confidently took on the task of feeding all those mouths and always said that none of her girls were ever hungry. The greatest sin one could commit at the beginning of term was to forget your ration book — terrible trouble awaited those unfortunate people. And parents were not too happy if we forgot to collect them from the office to take home at the beginning of the holidays so that they could continue to feed us. But the sweet coupons were our own. They were ours to keep. They were personal to us, and we could do with them exactly what we chose.

Everyone was allocated 12oz of chocolates and sweets each month, which meant 6oz each fortnight. There were D coupons which gave 2oz of chocs or E coupons which were equal to 4oz — and this was per fortnight. So one could have 2oz in one week, and 4oz the next, or save it all and have a splurge or even eat it all on the first day! The permutations were many. But there was no way round those 6oz, unless a kind parent tipped up his entire ration, as my Father did for my Sister and I. He never even *saw* his coupons but being a very generous man derived quiet enjoyment in being able to add to our ration.

Actually it wasn't 'chocolate' as we know it today. It was neither milk nor plain but a combination of both which arrived at the tuck shop in very large blocks. The tuck shop lady broke it by hand into some little scales. But we didn't complain — it was chocolate, although I remember lying in bed with saliva juices working and with memories of "before the war" we would recall "Maltesers", "Mars Bars" and

"Crunchies" and genuinely wonder if we would ever see them again.

One girl I do remember who must have had connections with the chocolate world. She seemed to have an endless supply of the most delicious 'mishapes' and we could hardly bear to witness her greed. Not being of a generous nature, she was fairly unpopular. Another slight help in the chocolate stakes was to procure a tin of Cadburys drinking chocolate — very scarce, but we mixed it with precious sugar brought from home, and ate it by the spoonful or in the palm of the hand in the absence of a spoon.

All meals were taken in relative normality in two large rooms. Two houses shared a dining room, and changed round each term. "Lower" dining room which was formerly the servant's hall, and is now the Muniment room, made an exceedingly adequate room for two houses and "Upper" was a little higher in location but, still below stairs. The staff who were not on duty with us in the dining rooms ate in the former Housemaid's pantry. It possessed an enormous sink at which the staff did their own washing-up of dishes. Usually with lukewarm water and very little soap.

Lower dining hall for Penrhos.

DINING ROOMS

Penrhos dining hall at Colwyn Bay before the war.

Each room had a high table, where girls were placed next to Mistresses in order to develop the art of conversation and good manners.

Manners were drilled in very firmly from day one. A girl could never say "pass the salt please" nor even "please will you pass the salt" — Oh no, one must "hint". "Would you like some salt Mary?" "No thank you, but do help yourself". After a few meals, this lesson was quickly learned and "Help yourself to water, salt, and bread" was automatically being mouthed everywhere — but it had to be spoken and we were soon into that particular groove as easily as swallowing. There was also in Upper dining room a French table which was not popular, as all conversation had to take place in the French language. It was noticeably the quietest corner of the whole room, except for the French Mistress who was voluble and loud. We queued cafeteria style for the first course but once seated we didn't rise again. The pudding was passed down the table and maids asked each girl if she would "like a little more?"

After breakfast and whilst still seated, the post was handed out down the rows, a much awaited moment. We became familiar with everyone's mail from home as we passed it along the table, hand to hand. We knew most people's mother's (it was almost always mothers') handwriting or the colour of the envelope.

After grace had been said, an even greater hope dawned. A list of lucky girls for whom parcels awaited, was read out. We collected them after lunch from 'Parcel Cupboard', where-in any food from home had to be kept. Mice were an ever constant hazard, so odd pieces of cake or biscuits were kept under close guard. A stout tuck tin was a most necessary thing to own.

There was an occasion where a nest of baby mice was found, comfortably ensconced in piles of knitting wool. We all knitted for the troops, and this little family had made itself at home in a desk in Stag Parlour, where the wool was stored.

THE BLACK-OUT

Everyone who lived in Great Britain during World War II have their own memories of the Black-out. The blacking out of windows of their home, so that no chink of light showed outside to assist the enemy planes. Many were the jokes about the Air Raid Wardens as they roamed round the streets and countryside shouting "Put that light out". But the blacking out of Chatsworth House was certainly no joke, to those in charge it was a constant worry and headache. Fortunately most of the windows had large solid shutters, so it was just a case of seeing that all the shutters worked properly, and were closed at dusk each night. "Black-out time" was an official word, almost used as we now use G.M.T.

Joan (Fazakerley) Kerr remembers how the Senior girls were sent outside to inspect the whole building for any specks of light. It was done on a rota basis, two or three girls together each night. They would go out of the North Hall, through the small gate into the West Gardens. Walk along the west side up the steps to the south side, and in at the east entrance near the Grotto. Thus they had seen all four sides of the building, and any sign of light was reported immediately. They found this particular chore quite eerie on very dark nights, especially passing the statues, with only a blacked-out torch to find their way.

Joan also remembers an occasion when the "black-out" fell down in one of the Painted Hall windows. We were all enjoying a film and the Earl of Stockton (then Mr Harold Macmillan) was in the audience. He was sitting with our Headmistress and was first on the scene to reinstate the faulty "black-out". Occasionally we would open the bedroom shutters after lights out, but had to remember to refix them in the morning. After all that fuss and bother with this nightly nuisance, it is ironic that when German planes *did* attack us, it was on a beautiful light Summer's evening!!

INFLUENZA 1943

During the lent term of 1943 the school was hit by a most virulent 'flu epidemic. Life seemed to stop as staff and girls fell like flies before an aerosol. The San, which even full to capacity could only hold 12 girls, was soon full. It was decided to make the large dining room into a hospital ward. I soon succumbed to join the latest bout of illness, and I could take you now to the very spot on which my bed came to rest in dining room dormitory. Whereas in the San in Cavendish wing, ages had been segregated and one was rarely confined to bed with anyone much older or younger than oneself, in dining room hospital ward there was neither time nor energy to consider such niceties. All age groups from 11 to 18 years were in it together.

My human biology education was forwarded during that time, as with ears pinned back, I eavesdropped on two Senior girls as they discussed men and sex (Not that we knew that word at all) I think it more than likely, that their knowledge of this subject was nearly as sketchy as mine, but I gave them my fullest attention as they talked.

There was quite a craze for the latest musical hit of the time, and two of the Seniors did a very good 'turn' singing in harmony the song "You are my Sunshine".

School work, and indeed school life, was heavily disrupted, and many of the staff who were still upright, took on nursing duties; but the pressure of the epidemic was so great, that several nurses were imported from a hospital in the area.

I finished my bout of 'flu in rather poorly circumstances. Due to the general pressure, and needing beds, I was pronounced fit to return to school life. On the eve of my fourteenth birthday, which was 7th February, I remember standing at the top of the North hall steps, and feeling dreadfully ill. Someone came to my aid, the temperature was taken and I was hustled back into bed. Never mind, I was reinstated in the San (proper) and was deemed to be so ill, that Miss Smith solemnly came to lecture me on the importance of staying still, and in bed; and I was in fact 'in bed' for the rest of the term. Now I could wave to the girls lining up to go to Church in Edensor.

Then on 21st February, my eldest sister gave birth to a daughter. I had received a special 'home visit' in June 1941 to be a bridesmaid at her wedding. (No white icing on the cake, and lack of clothing coupons disrupting the wedding clothes) So many of my friends knew all about the coming event. News was 'phoned to the school that Jennifer had arrived safely. Now I was an auntie at only fourteen years — a feat which not many girls could boast. My other sister Betty, two years older than I, and at school with me, had a special home pass for the day to view the new arrival. No such luck for bedridden me, but she came to see me that night to tell me all about the baby.

The scholastic side of my education suffered greatly during this time — my morale did not.

DYSENTERY 1944

Another rather nasty infection which invaded the school during the lent term in 1944 was dysentery, which in pre-antibiotic days could be a serious hazard. At first it appeared to be a normal tummy bug, accompanied by diarrhoea. Then it became apparent that it was more than just food poisoning, as most of the girls were really quite ill, with a fever.

Whenever there was the slightest sign of an epidemic, large jugs of antiseptic were arrayed in the bathroom and we all had to 'gargle' twice a day. I don't think it was ever proved if 'gargling' helped to stem the germs. As it now appears to be quite out of fashion, possibly we were spreading more infection than preventing it. But at least it never reached the epidemic proportions of the 'flu of 1943.

Nevertheless, in some ways it was worse. It was a "notifiable disease" which meant that the area "Medical Officer of Health" had to be informed — serious stuff. Furthermore, before any girl could be pronounced 'cured' *three consecutive negative specimens* had to be obtained from a local laboratory. It was those three negatives which made up the nightmare of one being released. Naturally, I had to sample this latest germ. It actually struck during Chapel, one Sunday evening. Literally "Struck" — at the beginning of the service I felt fine — at the end I did not.

After a few days of illness, most girls felt quite fit again. But the worry of obtaining those three specimens was an ever present nightmare. One specimen would come back and it would be 'negative'. Then after two or three days we could send another — that also might be 'negative', with thoughts of returning to normal in the next few days our hopes were absolutely shattered when the third specimen returned was found to be 'positive' and the whole frustrating process had to begin again.

It might be thought that we would enjoy our spell from work, but that was not the case. Isolated we might be, but we were not "officially ill' and work was sent to us and it had to be done. Actually, we didn't mind that, as life was quite dull and rather lonely. But the holidays were looming ever nearer and there was a distinct possibility that we would not have received those magic "three negatives" in time to go home. The last day of term dawned, and six poor unfortunate girls were left to rattle around Chatsworth by themselves as all the rest of school left for home and the Easter Holidays. I was one of those six and had to be prepared to spend the 'holiday' at Chatsworth. One by one the lucky ones received their 3 negatives and headed for home. In the end another girl Jane, and myself were left quite alone. Many tears were shed as hopes were built up and shattered again as those 3 elusive negatives evaded us.

In some ways it was very peaceful. A Matron or the Mistress on fire watching duty (which of course went on throughout the holidays) kept their eye on us and we could do exactly what we wanted in the House and gardens. Also one of the mistresses on duty decided that Jane and I should be taught the rudiments of 'bridge'. This she duly did and it helped to wile away several evenings. I found this most useful in the holidays. My brother John had been invalided out of the R.A.F. with nephritis, and I could proudly make up one of the four round his bed. So these evenings had been well spent. Nevertheless, it was the HOLIDAYS, all our friends were at HOME, and I had a pony waiting to be ridden.

Jane and I slept in the end room of the 'San' (Cavendish wing) next to the bathroom. In the middle of one night, I awakened to feel something moving on my bed. Further inspection revealed a mouse in my dressing gown pocket. (Dressing gowns were always left on the end of beds in case of air raids). This mouse was happily enjoying some biscuit crumbs. (Which should not have been in the pocket, so I was reaping a well deserved punishment). We felt bound to go and impart this frightful event to Matron *immediately*. She, understandable, did not appreciate being awakened at 1.30a.m. to hear such information — especially as she was just as frightened as we were. We didn't catch the mouse, neither did we get any more sleep that night!

Eventually, Jane went home too, leaving me to spend the last five days quite alone. For some reason — maybe the San was being fumigated — I spent those last five days and nights in East Attics. However, at last I had a room to myself, and spent many hours playing Beethoven's 6th (Pastoral) Symphony, which a kind music mistress had loaned me, together with her gramophone.

Once my Mother knew that I was absolutely alone in the House she decided to act. She set forth with her friend Mrs Chambers, and by a cross country route, involving three bus rides (no question of using petrol and a car) they arrived in Baslow, where they went to ground in a Hotel. Walking daily across the Park, they visited me for my last few days, rejoiced with me when the wonderful 3 negatives finally arrived, and carried me off home triumphantly, on three more different buses. My release had come two days before the beginning of the next term. I had spent three weeks and five days, a very unwilling captive in Chatsworth — rather like Mary Queen of Scots a few centuries earlier.

The joy of my homecoming was marvellous, and the school gave me permission to have an extra ten days at home, when the term had started. I remember my Mother saying to me without much hope, "Wouldn't it be a marvellous thing if you went back after two or three days when the proper term begins?" "Yes" I agreed. "It would be marvellous, but it was much more marvellous than I was willing to be". I had my extra ten days holiday at home, but went back to school still feeling a martyr.

FOOT CLASS

Another area of health in which authority took an interest, was our feet. Each pair was inspected by a doctor at the beginning of term, and those girls who were deemed to have flat feet had to attend foot class twice a week. This was a great bore but there was no way we could hide flat feet and equally no way of getting excused from "foot class". I never experienced this nuisance, but remember seeing rows of girls sitting on the floor in the West Hall where the classes were held after lunch. It mainly consisted of bending and wriggling the toes, ankles, and feet for about half an hour. It must have done some good because girls did eventually 'leave' foot class, so presumably they were cured.

HAIR INSPECTION

This now outdated practice was an inspection of our hair, with a fine tooth comb, for the purpose of spotting a girl who might have carried head lice in from the big wide world. Seeming now to be a rather archaic procedure, it was carried out in many schools at that time. "Hair Inspection" it was politely termed by the school, but to us it was "bug scraping", and it took place as early as possible after our return, either on the first night of term or early the following morning. A dreary beginning to the term, but we waited patiently in line for this distasteful procedure. A Matron with spectacles firmly in place, would part each section of hair, and peer closely for any signs of bugs. I never remember any girl in possession of these mites. But I do remember a Matron of Czechoslovakian origin. Her English wasn't too good, but she did have a sense of humour. One girl facetiously asked her "why can't we all wash our hair in disinfectant, and save everyone a lot of trouble?" "Oh no" she replied. "Dat would not kill zem, if you had them, zey loove a leetle swvim!!"

Paines stables and the hill down which we tobogganned.

Skating on Canal pond 1940.

Skating on Canal pond 1940, many more skates have been sent by urgent S.O.S. from home. Note the short gymslips always worn this length.

Frozen Canal pond and South lawn.

THE GARDENS

We were so lucky to be able to wander anywhere in the Gardens. They were a joy and delight to us at all times, especially in the Summer.

In the very cold, first winter spent at Chatsworth, Canal Pond (we called it Long Water Lake) was frozen. It was so frozen that we were all able to skate for many days, and frantic messages were sent home to dig into attics and cupboards to produce skates. Some were very old relics — mine were almost Victorian and were really too large, but most of us managed to equip ourselves with some kind of blade. Almost every winter there was enough snow for tobogganning, which we did with great gusto down the hill from the stables.

In Summer there really was no lovelier place to be. To be able to wander about alone, or with a friend, exploring, eating crab apples from the orchard! Studying for exams, or just sunbathing, or sitting on a rug and reading a book. Another world, how lucky we were. Only on one day of the year were the gardens closed to us. This was on one Sunday during the Summer term, when they were open to the public

Chatsworth daffodils in the spring.

Granville Corner — favourite spot for sunbathing, whoever arrived first.

in aid of the Nursing Association. Something about which I knew very well, as it was my mother's favourite charity. We were confined to the West gardens on this one afternoon in the year. The weather always seemed to be kind and as it was near to the end of term we were quite content to sit and revise for the all-important exams.

The Dowager Duchess occasionally showed American Servicemen round the gardens, and prefects were dispatched to make sure that we were not displaying too much bare flesh, during the hot afternoons. Senior girls who served tea to these interested visitors were much envied. There is a nice story about the Dowager Duchess, who was showing visitors around the House. They arrived in a state room, (then a dormitory) wherein was the four poster bed in which George II had died. This bed, being a permanent fixture had been left in place, and carefully covered in large sheets. The Dowager drew back the coverings, for the visitors to examine the bed more closely. Five or six horrified girls stared back from within the drapings. They had found what they thought an ideal hiding place to escape an afternoon walk in the rain. I'm sure the visitors were equally startled. It's not known what the Dowager's reactions were. She was no doubt amused.

The State bed which was left on site covered with sheets during our occupation.

The large lake which we used for swimming.

As soon as the weather became warm in the Summer term, the word was passed that we could start swimming. This was always marvellous news. For new girls a test had to be taken in the small pond in the West Gardens, before we were promoted to swim in the lake. This is the pond in the West gardens which is now laid out in box hedges, to represent the plan of Chiswick House. The present Duchess had this most unusual and pleasing idea, after viewing the old West Gardens and finding them (I quote from the Chatsworth Garden Guide) *"a very unsatisfactory muddle of shrubs... we planted golden box 3350 of them, as the dark climate of Derbyshire can do with any lightening that comes to hand... The design has to be looked down on from above to be seen as it was intended. It is meaningless, except for children to steeplechase over when you are on the same level"*.

Swimming in the lake entailed a very steep climb to the large Lake which is 350ft above ground level. The view from the top is magnificent (there really isn't a proper adjective to describe it) and very similar to that from the Hunting Tower. However, we hadn't many thoughts for the view, as panting and hot from the climb, we changed behind a convenient bush and plunged in. For those who were able to

Running round the pond in the West gardens before taking a test to qualify to swim in the large lake.

The same pond in West gardens in winter.

The same pond today with box hedges of the plan of Chiswick House.

The Cascade.

The Emperor fountain.

The Willow tree made entirely of copper.

dive there was a diving board, and although I don't suppose it would pass the hundreds of health and safety laws inflicted on us today, the girls thought it was wonderful. No one was allowed to swim too far out into the lake, and there was always someone anchored in a small rowing boat in case of accidents. But I never remember anyone having any difficulty. I do remember one girl insisting that she had swallowed a tadpole, but no one believed her and even if we had we would not have told authority. We had no intention of having this marvellous sport curtailed.

Occasionally, the fountains were turned on for our enjoyment. The Emperor, and the Cascade were two firm favourites. Shoes and socks were soon removed for a paddle in the Cascade.

Showing visitors the Willow Tree fountain or, as we called it the "Copper tree" was another great treat. We enjoyed their amazement at seeing this most realistic tree. It was made entirely of copper, by one of the earlier Dukes. After watching their reactions, we would dive behind some bushes into a cave where (sometimes) we could turn on a tap, and water sprouted from the branches of the tree. Their surprised cries of delight were everything that we could possibly expect.

The author (with dog) standing at the entrance to the Willow tree beside the moving stone (now wedged).

At the narrow entrance to this copper tree there was a vast stone which, when pushed, went slowly round like a revolving door in a hotel. One day, in a rush of enthusiasm and probably showing off, I crushed my right leg between the moving stone and the entrance. I duly suffered. I was in bed for a week and the bruising was most impressive. My leg still has a weak spot on the knee. The stone was immediately wedged, making it non-mobile, but we still referred to it as the rolling stone. Mr Link remembers this, and said apart from a small statue being dislodged at the top of the Cascade, the wedging of the 'moving stone' is the only 'damage' he can recall! It is still wedged today.

THE STATUES

We were intrigued by the statues, both inside the House and in the Gardens. Intrigued and amused, many a giggle was exchanged as we gaped at their near nudity, and I expect some of them must have given authority a few anxious moments. Sex education hadn't reached the over-kill of today, and maybe all most girls needed to enlarge their naive, vague and very innocent biological knowledge, was to live with the Chatsworth statues for a few years. But in the first arctic winter they looked so cold that some girls' idea of fun was to decorate these stone and marble figures with scarves and balaclava helmets. One statue which was a popular receptacle of garments was Mercury, at the top of the Painted Hall steps. It just cried out to be festooned by the odd bra' or B'B's (Bust Bodices as we referred to them in our laundry books). Authority was mostly amused rather than annoyed — it was quite harmless fun. Although if one was actually 'caught' doing it, the poor Mistress felt duty bound to dish out bad marks, but having done it once, the novelty soon wore off. I don't suppose the Chatsworth statues have ever had so much attention — either before our coming, or since.

Skit on statues from the school magazine 1940. Drawn by Mrs Jean (Brett) Reddaway.

OLD UNCLE TOM COBBLEY AND ALL!

Jean Brett

Statue today from the skit.

THE LATEST TANGO?

"THERE GOES MY ONE,
LONG LAST SUSPENDER!"

Statue today from the skit.

"WAITAH!"

The statues looked so cold.

The grand staircase and the statue Mercury, which we occasionally decorated with undergarments.

THE CHOIR

As a school we were heavily involved with music. Consequently, the choir played a great part in our lives. As we assembled for the morning or evening prayers, in the Painted Hall, those girls in the choir would collect a hassock from the pile at the side of the steps. Eventually after climbing and clambering over the bodies already there, we would all be in place, sitting on the steps and grouped in the four parts necessary for singing in harmony. Much pleasure was obtained by the girls in the choir and I'm sure they gave it to many people in the production of anthems and concerts.

The Painted Hall was a natural auditorium, and my father's fondest memory of the school, which he never tired of repeating, was arriving at the main entrance one Saturday morning, to suddenly hear the choir practising hymns. It was a glorious sound, we were drilled and tutored by three successive music teachers, all extremely able and dedicated.

One had to be a Senior, before being allowed to take a test for the choir. A most nerve racking experience. I was admitted, taking my test in

The view of the Painted Hall from the choir steps.

a tiny music room near the laundry. I was told my voice was considered good enough for extra lessons or "training" as it was known. These I eventually had and obtained my LRAM just after I left school.

Handel's Messiah was an annual event, and the school joined in the chorus. The soloists would practise these heavenly arias, alone at the top of the Painted Hall stairs whilst other girls were having lessons. If I could possibly manage it, I would creep onto the forbidden balcony to listen. As a Junior, I remember hearing a particularly lovely soprano voice singing "I know that my redeemer liveth". It was a thrill, and a privilege I will never forget.

But certainly my most exciting memory with the choir was on the last morning of the Autumn term when we awakened the rest of the school to the sound of Christmas carols. The choir assembled at the stables round the large trough in the middle of the stable compound at 6a.m. on that last morning just before Christmas. We had looked forward to this for weeks. No one minded getting up early on that particular morning, and in fact we hardly bothered to go to sleep.

We started singing carols in the cold, dark morning, and gradually progressed down the stable hill and all the way round the school. We were all so happy and excited, as we took the real spirit of Christmas home for the holidays.

GIRL GUIDES

Thursday afternoons were spent being a Girl Guide. It wasn't compulsory but most girls decided to join the movement. I promptly joined, attracted at first by the uniform but later I really came to enjoy and look forward to Thursday afternoons. I joined C Company and our meetings were held in the laundry. There were three companies, 'B' gathered in the squash court and 'A' in the theatre — all with different Guide Captains who were members of the staff. Immediately after lunch guide badges were polished with metal polish if available, but often with a surreptitious rubbing on the floor mats. Patrol leaders had scrubbed their lanyards earlier, and with a final polish to the shoes, straightening of the stocking seams, a quick association of nails and nail brush, and we were ready.

Chatsworth seemed to be purpose built for being a Guide. We never actually camped, much to my secret relief, as I never had any ambition whatsoever to sleep in a tent. But we did almost everything else possible. Tracking each other with sticks and arrows through the woods, with fire lighting and a camp fire at the end was quite a thrill. There was

Guides in the park washing up.

Crocodile in white, returing from Edensor Church. Girl Guides on parade in the background.

great scope for the numerous badges, available to be won; and some keen Guides soon had arms decorated like Christmas trees, with these colourful rewards.

A Cadet Force was also in being, only one company, but they seemed to do even more exciting activities, and sported a rather smart white tie. Miss Monica Beardsworth was the Cadet Captain and she writes *"It consisted of older Guides, who were training to be Guiders themselves eventually. This commitment was taken very seriously and the company meetings were geared to a large extent to preparation for the future.*

Studying the organisations of Brownie Packs, and Guide Companies and learning about the world wide ramifications of the Guide Movement, were all part of the Cadet's work, and although camping was impossible in war time, learning to pitch and strike tents, and generally organise a camp, was a regular part of summer meetings. It was a very happy and enthusiastic company and provided many future Guiders."

In 1942 we had the excitement of a visit from the Chief Guide Lady Baden-Powell. She was paying a visit to all Derbyshire Guides. We were still known as the 3rd Colwyn Bay Company, but as we were

Lady Baden-Powell, second from right, visits Chatsworth in 1942.

evacuated to Derbyshire, we were allowed to be the host Company; and we would also parade our world flag for the first time. Much time was spent practising so that everthing would be perfect for the great day. Unfortunately no one had told the elements just how important it was. The weather was appalling. Instead of assembling in all our glory outside, we crowded into the Orangery where the Chief Guide inspected us. Then into the Painted Hall, where she gave an amusing speech, telling us that she had been given her Silver Fish (a small silver fish which she wore on a cord) for "being a good girl". It was one of many occasions which we took into the future as a memory of our Chatsworth days.

THE STAFF AND LESSONS

The staff probably found the restrictions more irksome than some of the girls, although being older I'm sure they were able more fully to appreciate our unique position. To quote from Miss Monica Beardsworth's book "Penrhos College, the second 50 years" she says. *"Given the convenience of a private car, the position of Chatsworth is idyllic, but without a drop of petrol, as we were for part of the war, its isolation could at times be a burden. To get to any shops, apart from the tiny Edensor Post Office, one first had a long walk through the Park, then a jolting journey on infrequent buses, so that the outing required a full afternoon. This scarcely affected the girls, accustomed as they were to being immured at Colwyn Bay, but for some of the staff, the sense of being "cut off" was undoubtedly a trial."*

The younger staff and the prefects shared a fire watching role, and the rest of the staff were responsible for the marshalling of the school, and getting them safely to the Beer Cellars in the event of an air raid. Each night one staff and one prefect slept in a hut on the roof, while another pair slept in an alcove on Bachelors' corridor. Each pair had a telephone at hand so that they could be contacted by the Lodge and go into immediate action in case of an air raid or fire. In spite of these nocturnal interruptions, the staff were always on duty bright and early to do their work with the girls.

How lucky we were to have such teachers. I think I can say without fear of contradiction from any old girls, that we had one of the finest school staff in the whole country. From the Headmistress who was, and still is a marvellous lady, to the youngest, they all pulled together and made light of what at times must have been very trying circumstances. Their own scholastic qualifications were high, and they never spared themselves to give to us some of their high ideals and standards of work. I think the only strike they had ever heard of, was probably the General Strike in 1926 — as for "teachers striking", it would be as ridiculous to them then as science fiction is to me now.

All the various subjects found a corner in The House, and we changed form rooms for the special subjects; trailing along with books and gas masks, which at the beginning of the war were carried like a second skin everywhere.

Art was taught in the corner of the Orangery. It was light and airy, but draughty for the art mistress, and screened off from the dozens of lockers which we used for games equipment and clothes.

The squash court became the gym. Being extremely keen on gymnastics and having come from a school with bars and ropes. I remember the horror with which I viewed the squash court. How could we possibly manage in this tiny room? But we did, and developed great skills with the Horse, Buck, Box and Forms and eventually had ropes to climb and could still play "Ship Wreck" on the last gym lesson of the term. This latter was a form of harmless enjoyment and doubtless disposed of much pent up excitement towards the end of term. All the equipment was put out on the floor, one girl was pronounced "on", and we had to escape her touch without touching the floor, jumping from one piece of equipment to the next. The last remaining girl had "won"!

Domestic Science was taught in the rooms previously used for doing Chatsworth's laundry and ironing. Two fairly large rooms in which we learned to cook, and struggled to sew.

Private piano lessons were fitted in (literally) in the most peculiar places. There were four Music Mistresses, so many girls undertook this

The staff. Miss Smith centre front row.

Most of the school summer term 1942.

The Orangery which we used for art lessons, and storing games equipment, now the Chatsworth shop.

form of art. Twenty six pianos were placed around the House in any odd corner, for practising. Again, there was a strict rota for piano 'prac'. Although, for girls who were very good and keen, special arrangements were made and they could practise until a fairly later hour if the piano was out of earshot of sleeping juniors.

Fairly soon, several temporary class rooms of a modern prefabricated type were erected outside the Orangery, and these were a great help.

The Biology and Physics Laboratories took root in the kitchen regions. The Physics lab found a home in a room which had been the Butler's pantry. The pantry was situated next to the strong room, whence Mr Simmons the butler, made his way each morning. Here all the gold and silver plate was stored, and occasionally the physics class would be invited through for a viewing. He took an immense and loving pride in the gleaming gold and silver plate, which he spent a large part of each day cleaning. It was a continual year round task for when he had polished the last piece, it was time for him to start all over again.

The Biology lab was the former stillroom. In this room we could also organise a private Birthday party, from 4.15p.m. to 4.45p.m.! For girls who had a Birthday during the term. A cake was usually procured from home. About a dozen 'special' friends were bidden to share this feast, at the normal school tea time. The cake "was" the party, but those tea time Birthday invitations were highly prized. Normal "tea" consisted of bread, a very small pat of margarine and either jam *or* marmite, *or* peanut butter. Cake was normally reserved for Sunday, and that cake couldn't compete with one from home which had been lovingly baked with everything that was scarce and precious.

The Chemistry laboratory was more difficult to place. Bunsen burners and gas had to be laid on. It was not thought a very good idea to have dozens of girls experimenting with dangerous substances in The House. So the "Chemi-lab" was put into two rooms in the stables, together with a 240 volt power supply, as the House ran on 110 volts. In those gentle days before we were tyrannized by computers, laboratories were not the complicated nightmares of today. So we didn't feel at all deprived, and an Inspector for Education said after a visit to the school, that "Work of distinction" was being done.

Neither had language laboratories been born, I freely admit that I wish they had. But any girl who was really language minded had the

The private chapel in Chatsworth House.

Corner of the ante library used for private piano lessons.

best of teachers in both French and German. The German mistress was a native of Germany, but understandably German was a less popular language than French. We were all at that time great enthusiasts for General de Gaulle and it was definitely the thing to be seen wearing the free French badge. He encouraged it, so most of us contributed a penny a week to the "Free French" as well as the Red Cross.

Naturally, anything towards the war effort was pursued with vigour. We knitted for the troops (some better than others) but as it gained us some good points for our house we were doubly rewarded and our good points went towards winning the Handicraft Cup. We also adopted the ship H.M.S. Sheffield. We felt more personally involved when knitting for a specific thing. Some of the older girls wrote letters to the ship. I expect they felt very daring!

Throughout the country there would be a war week National Savings Campaign and we were encouraged to badger our parents to buy National Savings Certificates, which they usually did most generously.

THE THEATRE

The theatre also played a large part in the enjoyment of the school. Situated at the far end of the Orangery, one climbed stone steps to arrive in a fairly large room. To me it was a fascinating room; further stairs led to a gallery, where, I suppose, the V.I.P.'s of former days would enjoy the productions. As in all theatres there was a stage and 'wings' and there was a screen which could be let down when the stage was not in use. I have stared for many hours at that screen. On it was an old painting of Chatsworth and yet it was all wrong — rather like a transferred negative. Later I discovered it was an oil painting of Elizabethan Chatsworth by Richard Wilson after Jan Siberechts.

As well as the four house parties which took place, the biggest event was the school play at the end of Summer term. This was always given by the girls who took elocution lessons (also given in the theatre) It was rehearsed for many weeks and was quite a polished performance. "St. Joan". "The Barretts of Wimpole Street". "Vanity Fair" and "Pride and Prejudice" were a few which I remember.

Penrhos, being a musical school, had always arranged chamber music concerts and whenever possible instrumentalists were asked to Chatsworth to perform. We almost always enjoyed them, although I distinctly remember an occasion where our clapping was so loud with relief at the finish of a rather ghastly piece, that we were immediately given an encore.

The Theatre at Chatsworth.

GAMES AND UNIFORM

Games were played in an ideal spot, which was formerly the cricket pitch for Chatsworth. We used the very adequate pavilion for changing and keeping games equipment: Hockey, lacrosse sticks, cricket bats and other gear. There was room for two lacrosse or hockey pitches and two netball courts which we used in the Winter terms. In Summer, cricket and rounders were the order of the day and eight tennis courts were situated on the large South lawn outside The House. We trooped across the Park to play games three days a week, and had matches with various local schools.

The Summer uniform was a green linen culotte dress, combined with shorts. It was popular with everyone and would probably be welcome even in these fashion conscious days. The wide pleated "shorts" part of the dress made it comfortable for wearing both for school work and games. The lovely delicate, green Liberty silk dress worn for dancing class was a dream. Cut in Grecian style, it involved many yards of material and soon became impossible to buy with the meagre coupon allowance during the war. The Summer Sunday uniform was white; white hats, coats, dresses, and gloves. What an amazing sight we must have been, viewed en masse.

By the time we arrived at Chatsworth, clothing shortages were beginning to bite, so the odd navy Winter uniform coat was dotted among the virgin white. It was soon decided that we had better revert to navy only except for the white hats in the Summer term. Hats never needed 'coupons', so white hats could always be obtained. Sunday dresses were now navy for Winter and Summer, with detachable white collars and cuffs which were changed every week. Lisle stockings or sometimes even silk were worn with Sunday dresses instead of the black woollen stockings of the week-day wear. The navy week-day apparel was the usual school gymslip, and white blouse, together with the different coloured girdle of the particular house to which you belonged. But they were worn with a shortness that made the 1960's mini skirt positively Victorian. The knickers we wore were heavy black 'double-knit' with fairly long legs to cover the gap between suspenders and stocking tops. The gymslips were worn just about as short as a skating skirt and had it not been for those black pants we would have suffered with very chilly bottoms. But as leg-warmers keep the modern teenagers so ugly and warm today, so the black pants warmed our thighs, and curiously enough they were known as "tights" — with a convenient pocket in the knicker leg for a handkerchief.

Playing Lacrosse on the former cricket pitch.

Games in summer on the cricket pitch, pavillion in the background.

High jump on the South lawn.

Sports day on the cricket pitch.

Group on the tennis courts South lawn.

Leaving Edensor Church after Matins.

Group in West gardens 1943, author 2nd from right front row.

Nancie Park on same seat 1985.

There was a slight relief from school uniform. Every afternoon after games and before tea we changed into "home clothes". This sounds exciting and it certainly did give us a chance to show our individual tastes. But only up to a certain point. It could be a dress, or skirt and top, but each girl could only bring two changes, to last the complete term. This must have been a great relief to parents who had to juggle with clothing coupons, and it certainly meant that it curbed any tendency towards showing off by the more affluent girls. Later as the war progressed and the coupon situation became more desperate, other minor concessions were made and we could wear navy suits in exchange for the dresses on Sundays. But a white hat for Sundays in Summer (Navy for Winter of course) was the last remaining relic of the old order. Happily I still possess mine, together with its gold and white band.

One very horrid weekly task was that of "mending"; the mending of the weekly laundry. Especially tedious, was the darning of those black woollen stockings; they never seemed to be without a hole, as with a wooden "mushroom" and black wool, we cobbled the gaping holes together. All the girls laundry was sent to be done in Chesterfield. Every girl entered each item of clothing in her laundry book; then it was bundled into a laundry bag, firmly marked with her name and collected in vans by the laundry. The people at the laundry must have had an agreeable sense of humour; we often wrote little notes at the bottom of our 'list' and a usual one at the end of term would be "End of term, no more laundry, aren't we glad?" to which a message came back to us with three words saying "So are we!".

The laundry was always returned by Friday night and on Saturday morning in the class room "mending" took place. Armed with our bag of clean laundry and sewing basket we headed for form rooms, sitting at our desks to examine the clothes for missing buttons and for holes in the dreaded black stockings. As we muttered and grumbled our way through this seemingly endless task, a Matron would sit at the mistress's desk. When we had done what we thought was enough to get past her keen eye, she would examine it. More often than not, she was displeased, as her hand appeared through the criss-crossed black wool on the stocking heel or toe. But all things came to an end, and we would eventually report with much relief for school singing and "current events" in the Painted Hall. Occasionally she would take pity on any very young girl who was reduced to tears by this impossible task and finish it herself later.

SPEECH DAY

On Saturday 11th May 1940 Penrhos held its first Speech Day in Chatsworth. The chief guest was Her Grace The Duchess of Devonshire. She was a lady whom the school had already come to love and admire; not only had she received us so warmly into our wartime home, but she was noted for her sense of humour and we all looked forward to her visit on this unique occasion. Professor Warrington Yorke, President of the Council, introduced her to the school and I quote her entire speech to the parents, staff and girls.

"Mr Chairman, Miss Smith, Ladies and Gentlemen...

I feel it is a very great honour to be asked to come and give away the prizes here this afternoon.

I was quite overwhelmed by the warmth of your thanks for all that we may have been able to do here to make things more comfortable. You have been very kind indeed to thank us, and I know I am speaking for all who live here, and round here, and have had anything to do with Penrhos College. We thank you very much for your great consideration and kindness to us.

You might have made it rather frightening coming here, you might when we have asked for certain things to be done, which I am sure must have been very inconvenient, have made it look difficult, but never once have you done anything but treat us with every anxiety to make things as easy as possible, and if you say, Mr Chairman, that we regard you with respect, I can only assure you that we regard you all with the greatest affection.

Now I should like to thank the girls, because when I come over here and I see how you live, I think you have been very, very good, and the way you have taken on Chatsworth does you and the school the greatest credit.

If you have to thank me for anything, you have to thank me for making a speech this afternoon, for I can assure you that it is as great an agony to me as it is to you, and I have been thinking in those awful morning hours, when one is without apparent armour, "What on earth shall I say?" Well I thought that I would just say two things, (though I have, unfortunately, got my family facing me, as well as your kind faces). One thing that I think matters in education more than anything else,

Speech Day 1940 — left to right. Professor Warrington Yorke, Chairman of Governors. Miss Constance Smith, Headmistress. The Duchess of Devonshire. Rev. Prof. E. C. Waterhouse, The Dowager Duchess of Devonshire.

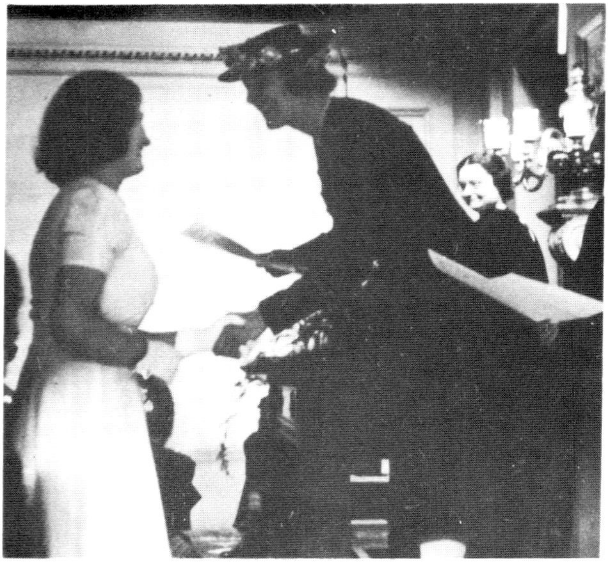

Speech Day 1940.

is getting the habit of reading; all your life it can stand by you, and be a good friend, but the only time that you can get this habit is when you are young. When you see, as I do, your children spending hour after hour reading shockers, do not think of this as completely waste of time, because one fine day they will be bored, but they will have got the habit of reading, and then they will read things really worth while. Read everything you can, and read with an enquiring mind and think for yourselves. It is a great nuisance to everybody if you ask a lot of questions, but do not mind about that, ask them. The people I know who have had the most interesting lives, are the people who have enquiring and original minds. I do beg you to believe that.

Well, I have only one other point before I sit down. I want you to think if you will, that perhaps your greatest war work, is to keep your standard of what matters in life, because, as has been said already, you are going to be the public opinion of England when the war is over, and it is very important, that that should be of the highest standard possible.

It is rather difficult when you live in the terrible times that we live in, to remember how awful it is to tell lies. Such terrible things are happening that the lesser things seem to get lost sight of, but after all, we are engaged at the present time in the greatest crusade the world has ever known since the advent of Christ, and all that we are doing, all that we are giving, the sacrifice that is being made, is to save these very standards.

Therefore, when you work here in the calm of a relatively peaceful part of England at the moment, try and make out in your mind what is important, and go for that with all your might. Say to yourselves, "This is what we are fighting for, and whatever happens this is what I must stand for."

Now I will tell you a little story. Last Summer I had the privilege of talking to a lady who had lived a great deal in Germany and had seen a great deal of their schools. One day one of the German Youth Movement Inspectors came round, to see one of the schools. He made them a speech, and at the end of it he said to the children, "Now children, what is the most important thing in the world?" Every child, except one, put up his hand and said, "Obedience". One child said "To tell the truth", and that child was brought up in England. Now you see what I mean. When you go from here, think out what matters, and say to yourselves that among these things are liberty, tolerance, un-

selfishness and good manners. Thankyou very much."

I have found that many girls have remembered that speech. I particularly remembered her advice about reading and found it to be very sound. Of all the Speech Days I can actually recall in my own school life and that of my son and daughter's Speech Days, this is the one on 11th May 1940 which remains most firmly in my mind.

PUNISHMENT

It would be interesting to compare punishment in schools today, with our punishments at Chatsworth. That we needed correction and were punished is certain, but my memory of it is limited. It could be that with time, all bad things fade. But I think it was rather the case that, as ''discipline'' figures so largely in my memory, it may be that, being over disciplined, girls needed less chastising.

The house spirit was greatly fostered. There were four houses, Raleigh, Drake, Shackleton and Scott. Later the names were changed, but the house system remained, in essence, exactly the same as far as it involved marks and punishment. These four houses, into which we were all divided, we supported with as much ardour as any young football fan today — minus the violence. Each term was split into four ''three weeks'' and at the end of those three weeks, each girl had gained or lost marks according to her endeavours or lack of them, for her house. Marks were given, or taken away for Games, Conduct, Neatness, Deportment, Handicraft, and of course ''Work''. For the house to win one of these cups was the main object of life from the beginning to the end of term. At the end of the school year, the house that had gained the most cups would win the coveted ''Rosa Hovey Trophy''. The finest and greatest accolade for any house and the main object of every girl and each house. So ''punishment'' mainly consisted of marks lost against the house, and if you were instrumental in losing marks, you were certainly letting down the side, and were most unpopular.

Collecting a ''signature'' (called by the girls a 'sig') was a disastrous thing and caused many minus marks. A punctuality mark (known as a 'punc') was thought to be less bad, but still a black mark. ''No, I didn't get a 'sig', only a 'punc''' was frequently heard. But a punctuality mark didn't mean that you were punctual, rather the reverse. They could easily be obtained for such things as the ''non humping of the mattress'' before breakfast, forgetting to do a necessary chore, and of course being late for lessons or other activities. There were good marks too, even for deportment. Girls who were seen to be walking round the school with straight backs suddenly found they had made their house richer by several marks towards the Deportment Cup.

The Neatness Cup was given in a similar way, neatness of ones dress, and hair, was rewarded, or punished. Also our dressing table drawers were frequently inspected by Matrons, whilst we were busy with lessons. We rather resented this intrusion into our clothes and treasures.

But woebetide any girl whose socks and hankies fraternized in an untidy way. As it was always a spot check most drawers were kept pathologically neat in order to qualify for the Neatness Cup. At the end of each "three weekly marks" a house meeting was held. The House Captain, (who, to younger girls seemed almost as awe inspiring as the Headmistress) made us wilt and cringe as she read out bad marks, with orders to improve next time. She could also be condescendingly pleased, and there were always one or two girls who left the meeting, basking in the pleasure of her praise.

To illustrate the earnestness with which we pursued the various "Cups", and the pride with which we remembered our "entertainments", I have reproduced a House notes from the Penrhosian Magazine 1940.

DRAKE HOUSE NOTES 1939—1940

"The traditional school entertainment plays as important a part in school life at Chatsworth as at Colwyn Bay; and Drake felt the honour and responisibilty of being the first to produce an entertainment in the school's new home.

Our film was "Jack of all Trades" and dancing in the theatre completed the programme. We had pleasure in receiving as our guests, Lady Elizabeth and Lady Anne Cavendish and Miss Bazeley, their Governess, and hope they enjoyed the party, as much as the school seemed to. Certainly if success is to be judged by pecuniary gains, we did well, raising in all £11.8.3d. which was distributed among various charities.

With regard to cups, last Summer term was the most successful for Drake. As well as winning the Work, Conduct, and Neatness cups which speak for hard work from the whole house, we gained through our more athletic members the Upper School Cricket and Swimming cup and Middle School Swimming cup, tennis prize and tennis championship. This is to be remembered as a record term for Drake and one worthy to spur us on to further heights.

With regard to conduct, the new climate seems to have made us a little too boisterous.......

MR WILLIAM K. SHIMWELL

We didn't suffer from over exposure to male company, in fact we hardly ever saw a man. So that it is perhaps not surprising that of the ones we did glimpse, they remain firmly in our memories.

Mr Shimwell, who was the Duke's Comptroller while we were at Chatsworth, was, I think, indispensable.

The present Duchess of Devonshire pays tribute to him in her book "The House", which was published fairly recently. I, who was the least important member of the school, personally remember him very well, and our Headmistress at Chatsworth remembers him with much gratitude, so I think he made a deep impression on many people. In his Obituary in the Penrhos Centenary magazine, Miss Smith, the Headmistress says, *"The school owed him a great debt of gratitude. When the war came he moved from his home in Edensor, into an office and bedroom in The House and looked after the Duke's interests and ours, simultaneously. To the ability and good-will with*

Mr William K. Shimwell Comptroller to the Duke of Devonshire during our stay at Chatsworth.

which he did this, we owe much of the smooth working of our stay at Chatsworth. Nothing was too big or too small for him to tackle. Burst boilers, flooded ceilings, fire alarms ringing in the night. He treated us not as invaders, but as guests, and took a whole hearted interest in the schools affairs." He also possessed a great sense of humour, saying to Miss Smith as some Senior girls left Penrhos for the last time rather tearfully, "Wet wicket today, I see!" It was an onerous task to have the ultimate responsibility for The House. But no one was more fitted to this job than William Shimwell.

Starting his working life at Chatsworth in 1908 in the kitchen gardens, he quickly became a Clerk in the Estate Office. He went with the Duke to Canada, as Clerk to Lord Richard Neville. Home again from Canada, he was made Comptroller and held that post until the late 1940's. He then retired from the post of Comptroller to become Clerk of Works, at which he remained until he retired in 1962. He was in charge of the electricians, carpenters, stone masons, upholsterers and even the laundry. In 1937 he was in charge of the renovation of the Painted Hall ceiling, and modestly refused any official credit.

I remember him simply because I liked him, very much. I was a small, and at first miserable little soul of 11 years. I'm sure he realised this and would always stop for a word if he saw me. And if he was anywhere in the vicinity, I made sure he saw me! He had a dear little puppy which he allowed me to take for a walk. I felt so proud. He realised that I adored dogs and it was his way of helping me to overcome my home-sickness. A very kind gentleman and admired by everyone.

After his retirement, he and his wife lived in a picturesque cottage in Edensor, where his great skills as a gardener were evident. When he died in 1980, he was mourned and missed by many people.

MR BERTRAM LINK

Mr Link was Head Gardener at Chatsworth from 1939-1969 and had just been put in charge at the beginning of our stay in The House. Coming from his native Kent in 1925, he remembers the time before the war, when Chatsworth employed about 40 gardeners. He started at Chatsworth as a young man of 19 years at 25/— per week.

Men further up the experience scale earned 35/— and at the top 38/—, a very good wage in the twenties. Scything could be done for extra money, paid on a piece work basis, and often starting at 5 o' clock in the morning.

All the flowers for The House were grown at Chatsworth. The only occasion Mr Link remembers 'buying in' was for the coming of age of the late Marquess of Hartington in August 1939. Then two thousand scabias were ordered, and other flowers in primrose yellow and Cambridge blue. Sometimes when guests came, he would make bouquets for the ladies and button holes for the gentlemen.

Mr Link recalls making a bouquet for Queen Mary and a button hole for King George V when they visited before the war. The latter always had a white pearl carnation. Chatsworth was famous for its carnations, camellias, and orchids. Wreath making, was another occupation. As cremation was not used as widely as today wreaths were often required.

By the time Penrhos moved into The House Mr Link had, at the age of 33 years, been promoted to Head Gardener. On his shoulders rested the responsibility of the 110 acres of garden, with a depleted staff. As well as keeping this vast acreage in order he had to tend numerous greenhouses where he grew peaches, grapes, carnations and camellias. Yet he was never too busy to have a friendly word and would patiently leave his work to cut down those marvellous peaches and grapes. He seemed to do it nearly single handed but he did, of course, have other avenues of help. He had several older men, two or three land girls appeared, and boys who were too young for conscription also came and went.

In spite of this (for Chatsworth) very small labour force, the gardens always seemed to be neat and tidy. Not much lawn mowing was done, clumps of heather came up on the lawn and a horse drawn mower was used occasionally. But the South Lawn came in for much more attention. In the Summer term the Chatsworth staff, (helped by our games mistress, Miss Peggy Bennett) laid out eight tennis courts. The mowing of these was done by Miss Bennett using a Ransome 30 inch automatic, an extremely modern machine at that time. Even so, this must have been quite a task, as the tennis courts were kept in excellent condition.

Mr Chester was in charge of the kitchen gardens which were situated behind the cricket pavilion in the Park. Quite separate from the other garden and surrounded in the proper manner by a large wall, they were carefully tended and grew extremely good produce. Girls from the school would go down to 'hoe' in their spare time. As well as his gardening duties, Mr Link was also a member of the Home Guard in Baslow — a duty which came easily to him, as he had been in the Territorials before the war. Mr and Mrs Link now live in Edensor and Mr Link still judges at local flower shows. He regularly plays golf on the private Chatsworth golf course just 100 yards away, across the road from his home.

MR FRANCIS THOMPSON

Mr Francis Thompson was the librarian and keeper of collections at Chatsworth. He came in the twenties and was in charge of all the articles of value during our stay from 1939-1946 and through the time The House 'rested' from 1946-1959. He assisted the present Duke and Duchess as they moved from Edensor into Chatsworth in 1959. He died in 1964.

A tall, extremely erudite gentleman, wearing a black skull cap, he was always there in the background. One can now imagine his horror to see 250 girls (albeit walking *not* running) invading this precious property. But he never gave any sign of his feelings. He had, like Mr Hovey, a quiet, gentle manner and from the day Penrhos invaded, he never spared himself in sharing with us his love of The House. During our stay through the war years, he was compiling a most comprehensive book about Chatsworth, and its contents. He wrote the Foreword to it in 1944, but probably due to post war paper regulations, it was not finally published until 1949. Called "A History of Chatsworth", it is now a collectors' piece, when it becomes available costing many more pounds than when first published. It is a solid, scholarly, tome of information, and must be a great source of reference for future generations.

When we first arrived at Chatsworth, Miss Smith remembers Mr Thompson handing to her a fire-proof bag. "In the event of an air raid," he asked her "will you save the largest uncut emerald in the world?" Actually she declined, thinking that girls were perhaps more important than emeralds! Miss Monica Beardsworth quotes, *"He knew every tiny detail of Chatsworth's history and of each individual item in his care. Occasionally he would open the Library into which we were not normally allowed, to show us the rare manuscripts and leather bound volumes which were to be found in this incredible collection of around 17,500 books. Then from time to time on Sunday, he would arrange displays of snuff boxes, of miniatures, and of jewels, elaborately and magnificently set. Each winking and gleaming in its showcase, had its own particular story, and Mr Thompson's young, fascinated audience were prepared to look and listen indefinitely.''* These show cases were situated outside Stag Parlour. They would be safely guarded, as Stag Parlour was the common room of the VIth form. The prefects, were quite a formidable bunch of girls and the policemen of the school.

At the beginning of the new school year, Mr Thompson would take a little trail of new girls round The House, pointing out the most important pictures and precious treasures. There would be a competition and small prize at the end of the route, for the girl who had digested the most knowledge. I never saw the end of my tour, I collapsed in tears, in front of the Henry VIII painting, which hung outside 'Den' bedroom and had to retire.

MR CLEMENT HOVEY

To Mr Clement Hovey, the school owes a great debt. He was Vice Chairman, and then for many years Chairman of Governors, and his two sisters were both connected with the school. Miss Rosa, was Headmistress from 1894-1928, and really built up the school from small beginnings. Miss Ethel, was the ''Lady Matron'' (we would say today Domestic Bursar) from 1895-1928, so he was very closely involved with the school. Affectionately known as ''Pa'' Hovey. (I don't think the girls knew him as anything else) He was a gentle, kind and quiet man, who spent his time 'giving' to Penrhos.

Always dressed in a dark suit and carrying a rolled umbrella, one saw Pa Hovey somewhere, almost every day. Sometimes in a corridor, or walking in the gardens, often carrying a camera. He moved from Colwyn Bay with the school, and took up permanent residence at the Devonshire Arms in Baslow. Nearly every day he would walk across the Park and was always available for advice. Nothing was too large or too small for his attention. Miss Smith, writing of his interest and help quotes a time when the school had returned to Colwyn Bay and was trying to repair the ravages of the Food Ministry during the war.

"Nothing but the best materials and workmanship satisfied him. I once queried whether he need have the bridge over the dingle repaired with such splendid materials, "If I didn't" he said, "It would be a light job. In thirty years it would need doing again." A 'light job' was a thing Mr Hovey abhorred, and the school reaped the benefit."

One other great benefit for the school, was that Pa Hovéy's hobby was photography. Film was almost unobtainable, but whenever he could manage to find some the school reaped the reward. The first arctic year is well documented; the Duke and Duchess have kindly loaned many of his photographs from their achives for this book. He also photographed many of the girls, both in large and small groups. A few days after this had happened word would go round the school "Pa Hovey's photos are 'up'". This sent everyone scurrying to the notice board outside 'Den' bedroom where they were pinned for our scrutiny. The board was soon surrounded by a hoard of girls each wanting to see their particular image. We could always order whatever we wanted at a very minimum charge. Had it not been for Mr Hovey, Penrhos' pictorial history at Chatsworth would be non-existent. His last act for the school was to give a stained glass window to commemorate the work of his two sisters. He went to the school for the last time to inspect the finished window on 22nd October 1954. Two days later he died — a great loss to many people and especially to the school to whom he gave so much.

MR E. I. HALLIDAY

In 1939 the artist E. I. Halliday painted a picture of the Chatsworth state room in wartime. It is a lovely painting, capturing entirely the atmosphere of the girls who slept in the rooms. The canvas was later hung in the Royal Academy and the Duke purchased it to include in his permanent collection and also generously presented to the school a full sized photograph of the picture. The original painting now rests on an easel in the State Drawing Room. And with his Grace's kind permission is reproduced on the cover of this book.

THE TRIALS OF AN ARTIST

A quiet afternoon in the State Rooms at Chatsworth 1939, after the style of Edward Halliday who drew the original cartoon whilst working on the Chatsworth picture.

As the war progressed and the threat of invasion faded, the school was kept informed mainly by notices on the "Current Events" board and by "Currents" on Saturday morning in the Painted Hall as not many girls possessed a wireless. Naturally, Senior girls were more aware of the war news than the younger sector of school. People throughout the country were expecting and then daily waiting for the "2nd Front" to begin. Everyone knew (although never directly from the news readers) that at last a great offensive was imminent to start the 'beginning of the end' of the war in Europe. So it was no surprise to the school when they were all called to the Painted Hall just before lunch on 6th June 1944 to hear the announcer on the wireless telling of the D Day landings.

I return to Betty Ley's diary. Here she is quoted at the beginning of the school year, September 1944, having just established herself in Stag Parlour (a room leading off from the Grotto) and the Common Room of the lower VIth.

"Back at school Sunday, 17th September, 1944. There was a huge Allied landing in Holland by paratroops. No place names have been given as yet. Being back at school, I don't know as much about it as I might have done... The landings were successful, except for Arnhem. Where last night we heard they had withdrawn. I gather there has been a pretty bloody battle, only being in this damn hole, I don't hear a great deal. 24 October 1944. In the papers this morning, it said that the Russians are on the 110 mile front in Prussia — Cheers!"

LATER IN THE WAR

"The war news at the moment seems to be quite good, I think. All the armies are advancing towards the Rhine. Gosh! it will be nice when the war is over, and everytime you stop to think, you don't have to realise that every minute men are being killed all over the world practically. And that Londoners aren't being given hell with the rockets. We don't know we're born here. Its only three weeks till we go home, thank goodness."

"January 30th 1945. The new Russian offensive has started, and they are doing things in their usual style, and today we hear on the wireless, that when the Russians get to Frankfurt, where they are fairly near to, they will only be 40 miles off the suburbs of Berlin. My God! I think the British on the whole want the Russians to get there first, because they won't spare any mercy. It has to be remembered, that although the '39, '40, '41, days were awful, the Germans were never actually on our soil, which makes an amazing difference really.

February 8th, 1945. Last night, getting ready for bed, it was the usual scene in Scots (a Senior bedroom). Some people just lying in bed, some reading, talking, and two of us putting our curlers in, and on the wireless, some variety show or other. When the announcer broke in on the programme by dramatically declaring that in London, Moscow, and Washington, the news was being given that we all paused and held our breaths. Churchill, Stalin and Roosevelt had met somewhere in the Black Sea — Phew! We wondered what was coming! Good Show!

This morning's paper says that 10 people have been killed in an aircraft going to the Conference. Fishy? and pretty serious."

As the war news grew better and better, and with victory in sight, it was now a question of "when" the actual announcement would be made that the war in Europe would be over.

The excitement in the country generally, was reflected in the feelings of all the staff and girls at Chatsworth.

As girls were scattered all over The House and Park during the day, it was quite difficult to decide how to let everyone know the moment news of victory came through. Not possessing a Union Jack, someone hit upon the idea that the next best thing would be a double bed (white) sheet.

Pat Laurie remembers that very moment. She was on the cricket pitch, actually batting, and making a 'run', when she spotted the sheet, which had been hoisted on to the roof of The House. Instead of completing her run, she grabbed the stumps, everyone whooped for joy, and the match was forgotten. Both teams and any girls who were in the Park flew back to The House for amazing scenes of cheering and jubilation. Although I'm sure no one thought about it at the time, the flying of the white sheet was rather significant. White flags are usually flown as a sign of surrender.

So, as the sheet was flown to show that the war was over, we were now surrendering our claim to Chatsworth. It would be ten more months before we actually left Chatsworth in peace.

ACCOUNT OF VE DAY CELEBRATIONS
8th MAY 1945 FROM BETTY LEY'S DIARY

"We began our celebrations, by having an extra hour in bed — always a treat at school.

We then had prayers, but instead of the ordinary routine of it, it was lengthened out into a short Thanksgiving Service. The altar was put up, with red tulips and white narcissi in brass vases, against the blue velvet curtains. All the staff were there in force, and the maids also.

The hymn was "Now Thank We All Our God" so appropriate, and a stirring tune. The Head gave out that we could go out in the morning, but had to be back for 12.30. It gave us about 2 hours.

Bucket, Liz, A. O. Setty, Marj, Podge, and myself, all cycled to Pilsley. We there bought pop. I had a large bottle of sparkling pop, which Bucket obstinately declares is intoxicating, but I'm sure it isn't. We then went on to Baslow — a glorious free wheel all the way. By this time it was pouring with rain, but we didn't care two hoots, and were thoroughly enjoying it. We all had macs on.

Bonfire on V.E. night 1945.

In Baslow we looked for food, but weren't lucky, and time was getting short. Every now and again, we stopped to have a swig at our bottles! Baslow looked gay.

Flags and bunting were hanging out of all windows. Edensor had done very well too, with a big Union Jack from the Church. As I took a swig from my bottle, some men in a van shouted "Good Health", and I said "Cheers", and waved my bottle.

We also got cheered by some R.A.F. men in the back of an R.A.F. van, and we waved our bottles back. We then had to go back.

It meant the long way round by Edensor, because they wouldn't let us in by the Golden Gates.

It was absolutely coming down in torrents. It was running down my legs, and into my shoes, and down my neck, but as I've said, we were enjoying it! We arrived back at school, and I was so hot, that I felt the bath was the only place, so I had one in 10 minutes before the lunch bell!

After lunch we were in the bedroom, hanging around until 3 o' clock, when we went to the Painted Hall to hear Mr Churchill.

The day was, on reflection, one of alternative feelings, one moment sober and quiet, and the next by being hilarious.

After the speech we played ping-pong, with books and tennis balls, and then ended up by playing rounders, and being thoroughly energetic!

Then at 5.30p.m. the staff gave an entertainment of Penrhos from 1939-1945, and it was jolly good. 1st scene, it was Colwyn Bay hectically making all the black out and then finding they had to move to Chatsworth. It was very funny. 2nd scene, was arrival at Chatsworth, Hartwell dressed as Apollo, standing on a pedestal showing disgust at the flying females! 3rd scene was fire watching and first-aid, and the 4th scene was the best. It was a skit on the school washing up and it was quite perfect! They did it all in time to Chopins Funeral March, and it was a perfect scream, I couldn't possibly explain it. 5th scene was called Nuts in May, and they were all dressed as different countries, and had Hitler and Musso, pulling all the countries he occupied away, and then Churchill, Stalin, and Eisenhower, pulling them back again. Quite a bright idea. After that was supper. They had put on a pretty good spread for us. Spam and crisps, and school made cake with marzipan icing.

I had to wash-up afterwards, and to my amazement, when I got there, there was the Head drying the pots! We all thought it was a very sweet gesture. She said it would help us to get through earlier. I had to tie an apron round her.

After a little while one of the housekeepers sent a maid to take her place, but we did think it was sweet of her.

We then rushed to the Painted Hall, again to hear the general Thanksgiving Service, and the Archbishop spoke, and the school joined in with the hymn.

After that there was a programme called 'Salute His Majesty' and first of all, his colonies saluted him. Canada, India, Australia, New Zealand, South Africa, and others.

Then the Royal Navy, who called him, their brother in arms, finishing with Rúle Brittania (and reducing me to tears).

Then the Army, Air Force, Civil Services, Nursing, also speeches from the W.R.E.N.S., A.T.S., and W.A.A.F.S. The Home Guard, and then a London mother, speaking for all the wives and mothers who had kept their homes going. It made me think of my mum acutely, because it was so typical.

After each of the former ones, they all played their National Anthems and respective Marches. Then lastly God Save The King. And then the King spoke. A very nice speech, and again the Anthem.

By this time it was about 9.30 and time to go and light the bonfire.

There was a dummy of Hitler, and a shout when he went up in flames, Liz the Head Girl lit it, from then till 11.15p.m. we stood round, making merry and singing all the songs we knew at the top of our voices.

It seems incredible really, that we could just stand there all that time, but it was fascinating.

We had cocoa and biscuits on the spot.

Gradually it grew dark, till at last, it was pitch dark and everyone's faces and legs were lit up.

They threw stuff on the fire to make it blaze up, and then Pa Hovey took flash photos.

The idea was to start up a song, and drown out as many people as you could, till everyone was singing your song and then someone else started.

It was grand fun. Then we all sang "Penrhosian All" (school song) and then went to bed.

It would be 12 o' clock before people got into bed.

We had midnight news. Churchill said that at a minute past 12 the peace would be signed. What a minute!

Then the reporters took us to London, Picadilly Circus and Whitehall.

I'm not sure whether we did go to Whitehall or not.

We heard the crowds cheering, they probably would make merry all night and some had been there since the early hours of the morning!

After that, they gave the weather forecast, which tickled me pink! Beginning of the war since I heard that, at the age of eleven!

That was one of the most impressive things I have heard to knock it in, that the war with Germany is over. Even now I don't think its really sunk in.

We were dead tired, but the Head had given us another hour in the morning.

So ended our VE Day.

Today Wednesday, we are carrying on as usual, and we are getting our other day, tacked on the Whit weekend."

TROUBLE WITH MINISTRY

The Ministry of Food did not seem at all eager to vacate our proper home in Colwyn Bay. Perhaps they had grown fond of the place, or maybe they didn't want to leave a town which had the reputation of being the sunniest place in the British Isles.

In the school centenary magazine published in 1980, Miss Smith writes of the trials and difficulties connected with returning to Colwyn Bay. *"Read the Parable of the Importunate Widow, and act on it,"* advised Mr Chuter Ede at the Ministry of Education, as we tried to get our own buildings released." I expect this is just what they did, and the Ministry finally moved back, from whence they came.

In February 1946, during the last term at Chatsworth, before returning to Colwyn Bay. Penrhos suffered another 'flu epidemic. It wasn't quite so disruptive or widespread as the scourge in 1943, but it was an added burden to those who were trying to organise the return move, and pack up all the school gear, furniture and books.

Most peoples' thoughts were now turning to the return to their old buildings, and the end of term was very welcome to those in authority.

However, it was with a great degree of sadness that everyone said goodbye to their wartime home for nearly seven years.

I quote again from Betty Ley's diary at the end of the last term.

"MARCH 20th 1946

The last night of term at Chatsworth and the place is chaotic.

Table, chairs, desks, beds, every mortal thing stacked and labelled, piles of rubbish.

Girls everywhere carrying trunks and chests, parcels and heaven knows what, and shall we be pleased to get away from it tomorrow, but the poor staff have the worst to come yet!

The removal of all these goods and chattels is a simply amazing task, plus the rubbish of the last seven years.

There is a certain sadness about leaving the place, and it really seems incredible that we shall never come back here, and when all is said and done we have had our school days here, and this is where our memories will be, and we shan't be able to visit the crimes of our youth!!!

This morning, I spent with Miss Hester and others, turning beds up-side down, and undoing the bits by stamping on them! There was then Mark reading and the Head gave us a talk on the behaviour of the school next term and impressing on us how we were starting afresh.

I'm so glad to be having at least one last term there... and the time for leaving draws nearer, and I like it less and less."

So, on 21st March 1946 Penrhos left Chatsworth for ever and The House was left empty — completely empty. Only those people belonging to Chatsworth could know what they thought and felt as they saw the last girls departing, never to return, and they contemplated the deserted rooms.

The school I know had tried to be careful; we had it instilled into us at all times that we were living in a very precious building. But 250 girls, and over 30 staff living for almost seven years in the same place must have left their mark. Just as we were welcomed so warmly and politely in 1939, no one was now going to blame us for any damage. I have tried from many sources to glean a little more information but have drawn a blank. I think Chatsworth people are too polite to apportion any blame to us. We do know that our combined breathing caused fungi to grow behind the pictures, and the doors were scuffed by girls feet.

I asked Miss Ilona Solymossy, who with her sister came to Chatsworth in August 1948. They were in charge of a working party who prepared the House for its first post war public visitors. There had been a gap of two years between the school leaving and Miss Solymossy's arrival, so she could not tell me very much about the damage. She was, however, very interested to question me on the subject of cleanliness. "Were we clean?" and if so, "how?" She could not reconcile the Chatsworth boilers of that time with over 300 females hygienic needs.

We do know that Chatsworth needed redecorating, but this was inevitable considering the length of time since the war had interfered with normal maintenance. So we may assume that we were probably better tenants than the British Army.

1880-1980 CENTENARY CELEBRATIONS

In 1980, Penrhos celebrated its centenary.

At the school in Colwyn Bay, the Prince of Wales paid the school a visit. He laid the foundation stone of the new Centenary buildings which included a lecture theatre, sixth form laboratories, new administrative quarters and a new entrance to the main building. He looked round, chatted to the girls and saw an exhibition of Penrhos through the ages. To me, however, a far more thrilling treat was in store. All Old Penrhosians of any age were invited back to Chatsworth for a reunion. My application was sent back by return and I couldn't remember looking forward to anything so much since I was a child.

On 4th November 1980 the day arrived. Those who wanted lunch (and I decided to do it in style) reported to two different hotels where, after far too long, we set out for The House. It turned out to have been a mistake to have lunch. It was after 2.30p.m. before we got to grips with the long awaited exploration of our 'old school'. Many sensible girls who ignored lunch had an hour start looking round. However, here we were, incredibly after all those years we were back. Every girl wore a badge.

Old Penrhosians reunion at Chatsworth 4th November 1980.

(With her maiden name if married). A lot of time was spent putting spectacles on or off (according to her type of eye), to read the names on the badges. Some people recognised each other, but mostly we did not — time and age had left its mark and names on the badges were most necessary.

Most of the time was spent in a frantic dash round The House trying to see all the old haunts but having to stop and waste precious time chatting. But it was a wonderful nostalgic visit, jogging memories and re-discovering friends. Many girls personal recollections of myself was "Oh yes, I remember you, little Nancie, you were always rushing about!" a rather doubtful way in which to be remembered.

I think it was because of that 1980 reunion at Chatsworth that old memories stirred and I wanted to record them for future years.

Whilst writing this history over the past year I have frequently visited Chatsworth. Everyone has been without fail helpful and interesting, sharing with me their time and memories. There have been changes both in The House and Gardens. The change inside, is of course more obvious. The school paraphernalia has long since disappeared and The House once again looks very grand as befits its status as (probably) the premier Stately Home in the country. It is now impressively filled with treasures and works of art. Some of them were neither there, nor in store when we inhabited the place but brought from the other Houses in the possession of the Devonshire family.

The largest change we see on the prescribed route for visitors inside is the reconstruction of Mary Queen of Scots Suite. (It was a Senior dormitory, known as "Scots" to Penrhosians). Small changes have been made inside. Rooms made into offices, different steps and entrances contrived, and the modernisation of some of the bathrooms. (Sadly Bachelors bath is there no more). Upper Dining Hall too, would be hard to recognise, but most of our old haunts remain in essence the same — even the lift, which still does duty.

The changes in the Gardens are not at first so obvious but any old Penrhosian will soon spot the four major ones.

The South Lawn, which held the school's grass tennis courts, now has two stately rows of pleached limes.

The Serpentine Hedge of Beech near the Ring Pond.

The Golden Box Hedges in the West gardens.

And the Maze has taken the place of the old Chatsworth hard tennis courts, next door to the school's House vegetable plots.

These have all been described in the official Garden Guide.

Parts of the stables are now flats, inhabited by Chatsworth tenants.

Another part of the stables has been converted into a unique tea room. This understates itself as visitors can not only have tea, but freshly made home cooked meals and refreshments.

South lawn today with the pleached lime hedges.

The old site of Paxton's greenhouse — now the maze.

Penrhos girls playing tennis on the site of the new maze.

Site of the four house gardens where we grew vegetables. Crab apple trees in the background.

A little way from the lodge, near the public entrance to the Gardens, one suddenly finds, behind the stone wall, comfortable cloakrooms. Warm and pretty with flowered wallpaper and pictures on the wall. (Both an unexpected but appreciated touch in this usually neglected room) It seems to be typical of Chatsworth's happy knack of keeping the nice things in life, without the usual modern intrusive practices. Hutber's law that "improvement means deterioration" certainly does not apply here, as Chatsworth prepares to move into the 21st Century. Happily, I could hear no piped music anywhere.

When I visited on a glorious Autumn day last October I took a gentle walk in the garden and arrived at the bottom of the Cascade, which, with all the fountains was active and glistening in the sunshine. I listened with interest, as a group of American and then German visitors stared at and talked about all the wonders around them. I looked down to The House, Gardens and Park, with the Emperor fountain playing on Canal Pond and found it so peaceful.

Nothing has really changed at Chatsworth. As it gave shelter to Penrhos in those dark years of war, so it now stands, solid as a rock, a beautiful, re-assuring sight, in this uncertain world.

South East view in winter.

South East view in summer.

Winter scene of 1st Duke's greenhouse.

Summer scene of 1st Duke's greenhouse.

Main drive winter 1940.

The drive where we congregated and made a crocodile for the walk to Edensor Church on Sunday morning.

Feeding the deer in winter.

The snow plough.

Frozen waterfall winter 1940.

Emperor and Seahorse fountains. The House in the background.

The Golden gates.

Bridge over the river Derwent.

Queen Mary's Bower (now used at the Chatsworth horse trials).

Canal pond in a quiet mood.